Remembrance

Remembrance
A Tribute to America's Veterans

Robert A. Fletcher
artwork

Robert B. Fletcher
text

Iron Mountain Press

New Milford, New York

Remembrance: A Tribute to America's Veterans. © 2002 Robert A. and Robert B. Fletcher. All rights reserved. No part of this publication may be reproduced, stored in a retrieval system or transmitted in any form by any means, electronic, mechanical, photo copying, recording or otherwise, without the written permission of the publisher except in the case of brief quotations embodied in critical articles and reviews. For information address Iron Mountain Press, PO Box 7, New Milford, New York, 10959.

First Edition 2002

ISBN O-9722961-0-7

Library of Congress Catalog–in Publication Data.

The Welder © Irene Carlisle, Used by permission.   The Battle © Louis Simpson, Used by permission.

Beginning of a Difference and Memorial Day © Rufus Collinson, Used by permission

An Iron Mountain Press book, Sales and Distribution Offices: PO Box 7 , New Milford, New York 10959

Iron Mountain Press books are available at special discounts for bulk purchases, for sales promotions, fund-raising, or educational purposes. www.veterantribute.com

Text by Robert B. Fletcher

Edited by Rufus Collinson

Artwork and design by Robert A. Fletcher

Technical direction and typography by Tom Lennon Associates, Inc.

Printing and Production Coordination by Integrated Communications

Created, designed and published in the USA. Printed in Hong Kong.

*Dedicated
to all veterans of
America's Wars
and those
who love them*

Chapter Contents

Chapter Six: World War II

Chapter Seven: Korean War

Chapter Eight: Vietnam War

Chapter Nine: Cold War

Chapter Ten: Persian Gulf War

Chapter Eleven: Afghanistan War

Chapter Twelve: Present Day

The Battle

Helmet and rifle, pack and overcoat
Marched through a forest. Somewhere up ahead
Guns thudded. Like the circle of a throat
The night on every side was turning red.

They halted and they dug. They sank likes moles
Into the clammy earth between the trees.
And soon the sentries, standing in their holes,
Felt the first snow. Their feet began to freeze.

At dawn the first shell landed with a crack.
Then shells and bullets swept the icy woods.
This lasted many days. The snow was black.
The corpses stiffened in their scarlet hoods.

Most clearly of that battle I remember
The tiredness in eyes, how hands looked thin
Around a cigarette, and the bright ember
Would pulse with all the life there was within.

—Louis Simpson

Foreword

The men and women who served in the armed forces of the United States earned our undying gratitude. As Lincoln said at Gettysburg, we cannot sufficiently honor those who gave their lives in that service. Living among us today are men and women of the same imperishable breed. Let us honor the American veterans, not only with words but with acts of loving kindness. Let us honor those who have been disabled, or are ill, or needy and alone. The care of Americans for one another was what made us a nation. The veterans among us are living reminders of our best hours, the unity of a people, the spirit that endures.

Louis Simpson, Pulitzer Prize winner 1992

Introduction

Wars between countries are catastrophes and they have plagued humanity for untold centuries. They have torn the very fabric of societies and cultures. They have wrought death, disability and destruction to innocent and often defenseless people. But wars have also brought out the best in human character. Faced with the prospect of annihilation, societies, and the individuals who comprise them, are forced to think more deeply about their raison d'etre, to martial every cell in their body to preserve and to prevail, to contemplate the prospects for peace and to build new institutions that may make future wars less likely. Actual warfare may be dehumanizing but it also unleashes great humanitarian resources. Given the horror and brutality of war it is often remarkable how quickly natural environments and human communities are reconstructed and healed after wars have ended and peace has been restored. Thus, while war itself is destructive it can also lead to positive reforms and transformations. Survivors of war yearn to put the memories of conflict behind them as they work to re-order and re-balance their everyday lives. But in the process, they strive to keep fresh their remembrance of those loved ones-family, friends, fellow citizens, and allies-who sacrificed their lives so that ours might be preserved.

In these starkly vivid and deeply human images of Americans mourning and honoring their veterans from the Revolutionary War to current struggle against terrorism, Robert and Rob Fletcher-father and son-have reminded us that the fallen guardians of our country must never be forgotten. Through these remarkable illustrations and poignant narratives we are introduced to the myriad ways in which successive generations of Americans have paid tribute to our war veterans. If anything else, this eloquent testimony will install in us feelings of respect and gratitude for our citizens in uniform-brave and patriotic men and women-and a sense of empathy for their families who have paid homage to them. I cannot think of a more fitting tribute.

Richard W. Hull

Dr. Richard W. Hull, **Professor of History, New York University**

About Remembrance

Remembrance was created from a desire to pay tribute in some small way to what veterans have done throughout America's history to preserve our freedom.

A loved one lost in war never leaves the hearts of parents, brothers, sisters, wives, husbands and fellow veterans. They live with their memories every day of their lives. Remembrance is meant to honor our veterans and gently help all of America to better understand what they have given. It is also a way for new generations who have known no war to learn both what veterans have done and the sacrifices we as a nation have made.

America's veterans are a symbol of our culture by their teamwork during times of war, their individualism as civilians and always their undaunted faith.

The word Remembrance was chosen very specifically. It is vital that we recognize our veterans, their families, and what they have contributed. They will never forget their wartime experiences. May we never forget them.

Bob and Rob Fletcher

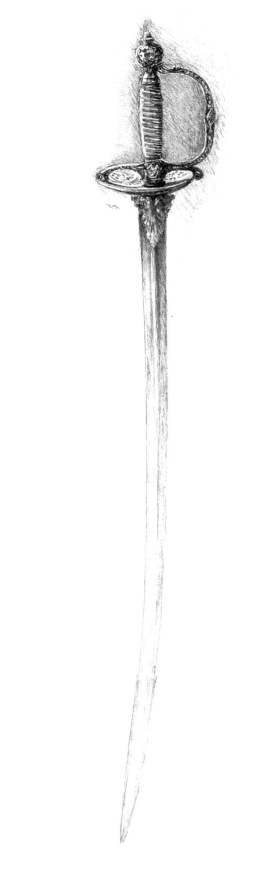

CHAPTER ONE: REVOLUTIONARY WAR

By the rude bridge that arched the flood,
Their flag to April's breeze unfurled,
Here once the embattled farmers stood,
And fired the shot heard round the world.

The foe long since in silence slept;
Alike the conqueror silent sleeps;
And Time the ruined bridge has swept
Down the dark stream which seaward creeps.

On this green bank, by this soft stream,
We set today a votive stone;
That memory may their deed redeem,
When, like our sires, our sons are gone.

–Ralph Waldo Emerson, "Concord Hymn"

REVOLUTIONARY WAR 1775-1784

The Revolutionary War brought about the birth of a nation. Despite being unprepared for war, with no central government, army, or navy, the patriots were able to beat the British. Lord Percy said, "there was not a stone-wall or house, though before in appearance evacuated, from whence the Rebels did not fire upon us."

Even though we celebrate the Declaration of Independence in 1776, the war began in 1775 in Lexington and Concord in Massachusetts and didn't end until 1784 when the British signed the Treaty of Paris, recognizing the independence of the United States and doubling the size of the original thirteen colonies. Almost 300,000 Americans fought; roughly 7,000 were killed in action, and approximately 8,200 wounded. This number pales against the number of those who died from disease, exposure, or while being held as prisoners of war: 18,500 died. Overall, 27,000 Americans were killed or missing, three times the number of British casualties. Soldiers came out of the war penniless or in debt, having served for little or no pay. The new government emerged deeply in debt. It wasn't until the early 1800s that the government was able to pay off its war debt and provide pensions for the veterans.

The Revolutionary War established the fighting, can-do spirit of young America and later inspired people in many lands as they fought for their freedom. As patriot General Nathanael Greene said, "We fight, get beat, rise, and fight again."

Dress Sword

Colonel David McCamly

The battle is not to the strong alone; it is for the vigilant, the active, the brave.
I know not what course others may take, but as for me, give me liberty or give me death.
—Patrick Henry

Colonel David McCamly II (1745-1817), a Revolutionary war veteran, is buried on the hill-top site of his 1,500-acre farm overlooking the Warwick Valley in New York State. The two distant mountains are Adam and Eve. The four small flags on the hearse have 15 stars and 15 stripes representing the 15 states – the configuration of the flag from 1795 to 1817.

This funeral took place well before the Civil War and the custom of covering the casket with a flag. The pastor, Bible in hand, leads the six pallbearers, including the colonel's two sons, friends and neighbors who carry the simple pine casket to the gravesite.

Colonel McCamly had been host to the first circuit rider in the area, the Rev. Ezekiel Cooper. Circuit riders were preachers who traveled on horseback from town to town. They provided the inspiration for the traditional blues song "C.C. Rider." Rev. Cooper was prodigious, often traveling from Georgia to New Hampshire.

Services in the area alternated between McCamly's home and the nearby Lazear Tavern, later known as "The Methodist Tavern." A tavern license required that the Word of God be preached there once a week. The family's religious ways continued with son David III – he donated the land and money to build the New Milford Methodist Church in 1838.

The wagon is a simple farm cart, the predecessor of the pickup truck. These rough wagons were often made by local blacksmiths in their shops. The hilltop shown here has been cleared to make charcoal to be used in New York City and to create a pasture for animals. When they weren't clearing their land, farmers cleared public roadways to work off their taxes.

Roughly a quarter acre had to be cleared for each mile of Indian trail to be widened enough for wagons. "Clearing" just meant cutting down the trees. Stumps, boulders and holes were left alone. A driver never left home on a journey without an ax.

Eighteenth century medicine was far from exact. Death came in many forms: consumption, fever, asthma, fits, pleurisy, and even hives. The Continental Army used churches and private homes as hospitals. Communicable disease spread rapidly. In 1777, the Army's stay in Morristown, New Jersey, carried with it an epidemic of smallpox and dysentery. Washington's troops were inoculated but the residents weren't; 67 town residents died.

Surgery in those days was essentially carpentry, with tools such as a flean (for blood letting) and a trepline (for relieving pressure on the brain caused by a blow to the head). Anesthetic was rare, and patients chewed a musket ball to protect them from biting their tongue off during surgery. From the Revolutionary War to World War I, more soldiers died from sickness, disease, and wounds than on the battlefield.

Gateway Lantern

The energy, the faith, the devotion which we bring to defending freedom will light our country and all who serve it — and the glow from that fire can truly light the world.
–President John F. Kennedy

Funerals were held at home in the 1700s. A lantern with a candle lit the gateway entrance to homes. A small black bow was tied to the gateway lantern to let neighbors know that a funeral was going to take place.

The lantern was made of tin plate – sheet iron coated with tin to prevent rusting. A tinsmith repeatedly heated and flattened bar iron in small pieces. Tin plate, or sheet tin, could also be purchased from England and was a stubborn, demanding medium to work with. Products using tin plate were endless; almost any vessel could be made – pails, candlesticks, funnels, coffeepots, colanders, foot stoves, snuffers, pitchers.

Lanterns had three or four glass sides often protected by glass wires. Some round lanterns had no glass. These incorrectly named "Paul Revere" lanterns had several hundred small holes punched in patterns from the inside. Revere would have had a challenging time seeing the light from one of these all the way across the Charles River.

Lantern glass was either made by German immigrants or imported from England. Glass, always in great demand, was one of the items taxed without representation.

Candles were the main artificial source of light during colonial times. As a result, people were early risers, and they made or bought a lot of candles. A big house might use forty to fifty candles in a night.

Tallow candles were the cheapest, messiest, smelliest, and smokiest. They were made by melting beef, mutton, moose, or even bear fat in a large iron pot on a crane in the fireplace. The fat was boiled in water until the water boiled away and the dirt was skimmed off. Wick strings, made of loosely spun hemp or cotton dipped in saltpeter, were tied to slender sticks. The family dipped the strings repeatedly in the tallow until the candles were the desired size.

Later, tin molds were used for candle making. A string was placed in each tube and then the tallow was poured in. Once cooled, the wax shrank, allowing the candles to be pulled out of the mold without being broken. Candle making was difficult, time-consuming work.

It is no wonder that many people preferred to purchase candles from candle-makers, known as chandlers. Ben Franklin's father was a chandler. A chandler and a helper would dip five hundred pounds of candles in a day.

After 1750, whalers started bringing in sperm whales. The fatty solid substance in whale heads was found to be the most superior candle material. It gave the brightest light (three times the light of a tallow candle) and never dripped.

Candles remained an integral light source until well after the Civil War. To this day, the light of candles symbolizes liberty, hope, and passion.

Muffled Drum

I hear the great drums pounding,
And the small drums steady whirring,
And every blow of the great convulsive drums,
Strikes me through and through.
–Walt Whitman

The beat of the drum and the lilt of the fife have provided the musical accompaniment to many wars, but none more memorably than the Revolutionary War. Every company had at least one drummer and one fifer for music and signaling. Some regiments had as many as twenty.

From reveille to tattoo, they sounded the signals of the day. They beckoned soldiers to come together, signaled when to strike the tents, ordered the march and the speed of the step. They called halts, mealtimes, church services, and parleys with the enemy. They even officiated when soldiers convicted of a crime were "drummed" out of camp in a mock parade. Soldiers' lives depended on the drummer and fifer to play their signals correctly.

Field drums were either snare drums or bass drums. Eighteenth century snare drums were larger than the modern day variety, ranging from 13-14 inches deep and 14-17 inches in diameter. Two hoops, added at the ends, held the heads in place, making the drums look several inches deeper. Ropes, along with sliding leather tugs for tightening, were laced through holes in the hoops. The snare on the bottom was made of gut strands. These strands were loosened to create a muffled sound for funeral marches. Bass drums, roughly 24 inches deep and 22 inches in diameter, were carried across the chest and beaten with two wooden strikers.

The fife of the Revolutionary War period was usually made of a hard, close-grained wood such as boxwood and did not have a mouthpiece. Some fifes of the time may have been made from iron; one found in Colonial Williamsburg was cut from the barrel of a musket. Settlers and soldiers from Europe brought the fife to America. Particularly suited to the jigs and reels of the time, the fife was extremely popular in the 18th and 19th century and was a natural for patriotic parades.

Most Revolutionary War songs and poetry were written (in true American fashion) by little-known or unknown men. The most famous song to come out of the Revolution was "Yankee Doodle." It was written by the British to mock the Americans; in fact the British played it as they marched from Boston to Concord. The colonials soon took it as their own and added an incalculable number of verses. A character in Royall Tyler's play *The Contrast* (1787) boasts that while he "only knows 190 of the verses, my sister Tabitha can sing them all."

While traveling with Washington's army, Thomas Paine wrote one of his most famous essays using a drum-head for a desk and a campfire for light. The poignancy of the journey resonates in his words: "These are the times that try men's souls. The summer soldier and sunshine patriot will, in this crisis, shrink from the service of his country; but he that stands it now deserves the love and thanks of man and woman. Tyranny, like hell, is not easily conquered."

Henry Wadsworth Longfellow wrote that, "Art is long, and time is fleeting, and our hearts, though stout and brave, still, like muffled drums, are beating funeral marches to the grave."

CHAPTER TWO: WAR OF 1812

All to revenge, to Maryland they came,
And costly works of art assail'd with flame;
In Washington they left a dismal void,
Poor compensation for their ships destroy'd.

We burn, where guns their frigates poorly guard;
They burn, where scarce a gun is seen or heard!
–Phillip Freneau, "On the English Devastations at the City of Washington"

WAR OF 1812 1812-1815

The War of 1812 was probably the strangest battle America has ever fought. It began on June 18, 1812 with America declaring war on Great Britain two days after England repealed the laws that were the main reason for the fighting. Because of slow overseas communications, the United States did not learn of this until weeks after the war began. It is the only war in which Washington, D.C., was attacked and burned. The war, over free use of the seas, began with the United States invading Canada.

The final battle and only real American victory took place in 1815 in New Orleans 15 days after a peace treaty had been signed in Europe. Again, news arrived too late. The treaty itself never mentioned any of the issues that were the initial cause of the fighting and returned all captured land and restored all conditions to the way they were before the war. Unsurprisingly, both sides claimed victory.

America had been angry since the Revolutionary War over the failure of England to withdraw from American territory along the Great Lakes, and of Great Britain's backing of Indians in America's frontiers. The tipping point was England's policy of impressment, boarding American ships and seizing British sailors who had left the Navy and often American sailors as well and impressing them into the British Navy.

Burning of Washington, D.C.

Embargos failed miserably, almost ruining the New England shipping industry and severely hurting Southern planters. President James Madison, under severe opposition, signed a declaration of war in 1812. America was woefully unprepared; in 1812 there were barely 3,000 soldiers and only 172 officers in the entire armed forces. A three-pronged attack on Canada was launched, but was uncoordinated and failed miserably.

The war at sea was considerably more successful. The U.S. hired privateers – privately owned, armed ships – to fight. Between the privateers and the U.S. Navy, they captured or sunk about 1,500 British ships. In 1814 a small British force drove a panicky U.S. Army out of Washington, D.C. and set fire to the White House and the Capitol.

General Andrew Jackson led the U.S. forces to their only real major victory in New Orleans. Artillery and sharpshooters killed more than 1,500 British and lost few of their own men. Of course, this was a few weeks after the war had ended. However, the timing of the victory and news of the treaty led most Americans to mistakenly believe that they had won the War of 1812.

Several interesting pieces of Americana resulted from the War of 1812. The famous Old Ironsides ship located in Boston Harbor played a role in some of the major battles. The expression "don't give up the ship" comes from the last words of U.S. Navy hero James Lawrence. And Francis Scott Key wrote "The Star-Spangled Banner," inspired by the defense of Fort McHenry in Baltimore after the British had taken Washington.

CHAPTER THREE: CIVIL WAR

Dear Sarah,

The indications are very strong that we shall move in a few days, perhaps tomorrow. And lest I should not be able to write you again, I feel impelled to write a few lines that may fall under your eye when I am no more.

I have no misgivings about, or lack of confidence in the cause in which I am engaged, and my courage does not halt or falter. I know how American civilization now leans upon the triumph of the government, and how great a debt we owe to those who went before us through the blood and suffering of the Revolution. And I am willing, perfectly willing, to lay down all my joys in this life to help maintain this government, and to pay that debt.

Sarah, my love for you is deathless. It seems to bind me with mighty cables that nothing but omnipotence can break. And yet my love of country comes over me like a strong wind, and bears me irresistibly with all those chains to the battlefield.

If I do not return, my dear Sarah, never forget how much I loved you, nor that when my last breath escapes me on the battlefield, it will whisper your name. ... But, oh Sarah, if the dead can come back to this earth and flit unseen around those they love, I shall always be with you in the brightest day and the darkest night. Always. Always. And when the soft breeze fans your cheek, it shall be my breath. Or the cool air, your throbbing temple, it shall be my spirit passing by. Sarah, do not mourn me dead. Think I am gone, and wait for me. For we shall meet again.

–Sullivan Ballou, a major in the 2nd Rhode Island Volunteers, in a letter to his wife.
He died a week later, July 21, 1861, at the First Battle of Bull Run.

CIVIL WAR 1861-1865

More than three million Americans wore the blue and gray uniforms from 1861 to 1865, often brother pitted against brother, in the bloodiest war America had ever fought. As many as 24,000 soldiers died in one day, and more soldiers died – well over half a million – than all American forces lost in World War I and II combined.

In the end, however, the Union was preserved. The United States would remain indivisible. All Americans were guaranteed citizenship and voting rights, and four million slaves started new lives as free people.

The last war to be fought entirely on American soil, the Civil War was burned into the psyche of Americans in both the North and South, and redefined how we perceived ourselves as a nation.

The last Civil War veteran, John Salling, died in 1958 at age 112.

The Coachman

Left Behind

Now close all the windows and hush all the fields:
If the trees must, let them silently toss; No bird is singing now,
and if there is, be it my loss.
–Robert Frost, "Now Close the Windows"

A basket stands empty on a gristmill floor, symbolizing all that was left behind as volunteers throughout the North and South left home, family, and work to fight in the Civil War. Men of both sides were willing to lay down their lives for what they thought was right. Southerners fought for state rights and a society built economically upon human slavery. Northern volunteers fought to preserve the Union, even if many were unsure whether they opposed slavery.

Lincoln's proclamation called for 75,000 troops. Most of the responses, especially from Massachusetts, were immediate and enthusiastic. For example, three rifle companies were formed in one day in Milwaukee. Michigan cities gave $100,000 to buy equipment for the first troops.

Not all responses were positive, however, particularly from border states. "You can get no troops from North Carolina," proclaimed the governor. Missouri declared the requisition, "illegal, unconstitutional, and revolutionary in its object, inhuman and diabolical, and cannot be complied with."

Tennessee promised troops instead to the South, "50,000 if necessary, for the defense of our rights and those of our southern brethren."

Kentucky would supply no troops "for the wicked purpose of subduing her sister Southern states."

In every crossroads town, every city, rallies were held, and fifes and drums played. War spirit was in the air and men signed the volunteer musters. Abraham Lincoln told his Federal troops, "You are green, it is true; but they are green also. You are all green alike."

The Federal Army numbered only 16,000 in early 1861, spread mostly along the western border to fight the Indians. The Confederacy was newly formed. It was clear – this would be a war fought by volunteers.

Josiah Fitch Murphey of Massachusetts wrote in his memoirs that when he arrived in Boston by steamer, he and his comrades sang, "I'm a raw recruit with a brand new suit; One hundred dollars bounty; I'm going down to Washington, to fight for Nantucket County."

Massachusetts supplied the first volunteer troops of the North and were the first to head to Washington in response to Lincoln's call to defend the capital. These troops ran into trouble when they entered Maryland, where Southern sympathizers attacked them. The 6th Massachusetts Regiment suffered the war's first casualties; four men were killed. The others continued on to Washington and were greeted with tremendous cheers – the only troops to make it through and defend the Capitol for the coming week of isolation.

Lincoln said, "I don't believe there is any North. The Seventh Regiment is a myth. You are the only Northern realities." In the summer of 1861, Congress authorized 500,000 volunteers to be called up. Massachusetts continued to exceed its quota.

Both North and South, in different stages of preparation, sent their amateur armies off to war. As Douglas MacArthur later said, "The outfit soon took on color, dash and a unique flavor which is the essence of that elusive and deathless thing called soldiering."

Caring Hands

And they who for their country die shall fill an honored grave,
For glory lights the soldier's tomb, and beauty weeps the brave.
–Joseph Rodman Drake

Members of the 2nd Cavalry unit say farewell to one of their own. Military units were mostly made up of neighbors and friends who volunteered together. New York was responsible for the first volunteer cavalry regiment from the North during the Civil War, beginning in August, 1861. At first, the ill-trained Union cavalry were no match for the superior Confederate horsemen. Cavalry was always the most difficult force to prepare adequately for war. Long months were needed to find men comfortable with horses and for them to be trained properly. It was common knowledge that until he had two years of experience, a cavalryman was almost worthless.

This all changed as the war progressed. The epic battle at Gettysburg was a turning point for both the cavalry and the rest of the Union Army. The cavalrymen were finally properly trained and had some years of battle experience. General Custer, long before his infamous last stand, had this to say about his beloved cavalry, "I challenge the annals of warfare to produce a more brilliant or successful charge of cavalry than the one just recounted."

Their role continued to expand throughout the rest of the war. Major McClelland, staff member of the famous confederate cavalryman J.E.B. Stuart, said at the end of the war, "No branch of the Union Army contributed so much to the overthrow of Lee's army as the cavalry. But for the efficiency of this force it is safe to say that the war would have been indefinitely postponed."

Cavalrymen wore a sky blue over-coat with a stand-and-fall collar. It was double-breasted and had two rows of brass buttons in the front. A blue cape lined with yellow was attached under the coat collar. The Union hats, known as kepis, or forage hats, were dark blue with a chin strap usually kept above the brim. The kepi had gold-embroidered crossed saber insignias and the regimental number. The color yellow or gold anywhere on their uniforms stood for cavalry, as did the crossed sabers. The kepis were actually impractical for warfare and veteran soldiers could be seen wearing a floppy black felt hat instead during battle. The Confederates knew they were in for a real battle when they saw floppy black hats on the other side of enemy lines.

Every unit had a scout. He wore civilian clothes for his covert role. He gathered intelligence on enemy troop movements, supplies, trains, ammunition stores and terrain. He was iron-nerved, crossing enemy lines repeatedly and even mingling with enemy soldiers in enemy camps. The scout for this unit is shown wearing a beige up-turned hat.

The horse-drawn hearse shown here has extensive woodcarvings, beveled glass, wheels with rubber outer rims and ornate drapery. The flag is tied with a simple horseman's rope to keep it from blowing away.

5th Avenue, Manhattan

The boast of heraldry, the pomp of power, And all that beauty, all that wealth, e'er gave,
Await, alike, th' invisible hour; – "The paths of glory lead but to the grave."
—Thomas Gray, "Elegy Written in a Country Church Yard"

On a bright winter morning at the end of the nineteenth century, a funeral procession casts deep shadows in the snow as it moves south on Fifth Avenue. The carriages pass Central Park on one side and one of the city's many beautiful stone churches on the other. The driver and undertaker wear top hats and long coats. The front carriages are pulled by teams of matching black horses blanketed against the cold. The second coach carries the six pallbearers and is followed by carriages containing family and other mourners.

The 1800s saw remarkable changes in New York City. Manhattan's 11,400 acres were first surveyed by John Randel Jr. Some areas were so thickly wooded they were "impassable without the aid of an ax." When the terrain wasn't an obstacle, the squatters were, unleashing dogs, cabbages and artichokes on Randel and his men.

From Randel's 1810 survey came a revolutionary plan, calling for a grid with twelve avenues a hundred feet wide traveling north and south. Every two hundred feet there was to be a fifty-or sixty-foot-wide street at right angles.

Central Park was created in 1853 when eminent domain was used to take 778 acres (expanded to 843 a decade later) from almost 600 owners. Nearly two thousand "vagabonds and scoundrels" who squatted on the land were evicted in 1857, and Frederick Law Olmstead was hired to design the "lungs of the city." By 1859, almost four thousand men were clearing the land that was to become Central Park.

New York City in 1861 was for the most part opposed to the Civil War. Often called "the queen city of the South" because of its extensive trading with the Confederacy, it lost roughly half a billion dollars when the South defaulted on its loans during secession.

Unlike Massachusetts, New York lagged in recruits. The Conscription Act, which allowed young men to pay $300 to avoid military service, enraged the working class. The Draft Riots of 1863 resulted in the deaths of at least 400 men at the hands of the police or the military, and more than a million dollars of property damage.

Fifth Avenue is roughly the route taken by George Washington and his retreating troops when the British captured the city in the Revolutionary War. Before 1848, few houses were above 23rd Street. Four years later, the buildings stretched to 37th Street, and the names Astor and Vanderbilt became synonymous with gilt and ostentation.

It wasn't until the 1880s and 1890s that the opulent houses reached the 72nd Street. By the 1920s most of the lavish private homes had given way to luxury apartment houses.

Most nineteenth-century men traveled by saddle horse between home and office. On Sundays the roads were crowded with surreys, buggies, carriages, and coaches. In 1910, 300,000 horses were listed for non-farm use in New York City, with about three million listed throughout the nation. Hence the term "one-horse town."

Motorization soon changed the face of travel everywhere. By 1907, the age of the horse-drawn carriage in Manhattan was ending.

Confederate Burial

Let us cross over the river and rest under the shade of the trees.
—Stonewall Jackson's dying words, May 10, 1863

Dusk falls, creating long shadows as an undertaker, his assistant and two grave-diggers prepare to return to their village in rural Georgia at the Civil War's end. The assistant is lighting the lamps. The hearse is small, pulled by one horse; it is a wagon with an enclosed, windowed rear and side lamps.

By November, 1864, Brigadier-General William Tecumseh Sherman and the Union Army had taken Atlanta, burned most of it, and ordered its inhabitants to leave. His reply to pleas and protests was, "You might as well appeal against the thunderstorm."

With 62,000 men, he marched toward Savannah and the sea, promising, "I can make Georgia howl!" The army fanned out 60 miles wide and laid waste to everything it touched. On December 10, Sherman and his troops reached Savannah. Three days later, he took Fort McAllister and on December 22, Sherman wrote a telegram to President Lincoln: "I beg to present to you as a Christmas gift the city of Savannah, with 150 heavy guns and plenty of ammunition, also about 25,000 bales of cotton."

With fewer than 2200 casualties, Sherman had destroyed most of the resources of the South, and struck a great blow to its spirit.

The flag placed on the grave is a Confederate "battle flag," and although most Americans identify it with the South, it was never an official flag. The "Stars and Bars," which was the official flag of the Confederated States of America, was too similar to the Northern flag, and the two often were mistaken for each other on the battlefield. The rebels adopted the "Southern Cross" flag in 1861. It was red with a blue cross and 12 stars, 11 stars for the states in the CSA and one for Missouri, which had seceded but was not yet admitted.

In 1862, the stars were upped to 13 to reflect the 13 states in the CSA. The Southern Cross flag came in three sizes: infantry had the largest; artillery used the middle size and cavalry had the smallest. This made it easier for commanders to tell the location of various units. The battle flag was always in the front of the regiment so that soldiers knew where they should be.

Records are unclear as to how many served and died in the Southern armies. Historians estimate that 750,000 men served, of which a third died. Two to three times as many Confederates died of disease, specifically typhoid, smallpox and dysentery, than on the battlefield.

A Union officer said, "It is impossible to exaggerate the fierce energy with which the Confederate soldiers fought with what seemed like the very madness of despair."

Perhaps the fighting spirit of the Southern soldiers, with their Rebel yell, is best summed up by the inscription on the Confederate Memorial in Arlington Cemetery: "Not for fame or reward, not for place or for rank, not lured by ambition, or goaded by necessity, but in simple obedience to duty as they understood it, these men suffered all, sacrificed all, dared all, and died."

Eight Veterans

Battle is a joyous thing. … A sweet exultation rises in our hearts, in the feeling of our loyalty to each other. In seeing a friend so bravely risking his life in order to fulfill the commandment of our Creator, we resolve to go forward and live or die with him.
–Jean de Brueil, French knight, 1465

Six pallbearers and the officer in charge place the body of a member of their Ohio artillery unit into a horse-drawn hearse. The flag draping the casket has thirty-four stars and thirteen stripes.

Hearses were ornate, with beveled glass panels, velvet drapery, natural wood interiors, and canvas canopies that could be raised or lowered, depending on the weather. Side oil lamps were lit when traveling to the cemetery or at night. These hearses were extremely heavy. The brakes were attached to the rear wheels and operated by the driver.

The hearse was drawn by a team of horses of matching size and color with dark gray or black woolen blankets to protect the team from the snow and ice and to help regulate their body temperatures. The blankets were buckled around their chests and under their tails and covered them from the back of their ears to the tail.

Ohio was the only state to issue the brown coats and capes shown in the painting. Despite the popular notion that the North always wore blue, the Union Army, in a desperate rush to get units clothed, issued a variety of colors. The Seventh New York State Militia started the war in gray. As time passed, colors shifted from dark blue to black and brown.

Nonetheless, the standard issue from 1851 on was a sky-blue, single-breasted, kersey overcoat for enlisted troops. It was fastened with five buttons, and a short six-button cape lined in dark blue was attached to it. Officers were issued dark blue coats, but usually wore the sky-blue enlisted-man coat in battle to make themselves less visible. The officers' coats had four black silk frogs across the chest and a number of black silk braids on each cuff indicating the rank. These coats and capes were one of the few items available for protection against inclement weather.

Most Civil War veterans lived long after the Civil War and many saw the dawn of the 20th century. Walt Whitman celebrated veterans from both the Revolutionary War and the Civil War in his poetry, calling them a "race of veterans – race of victors! Race of the soil, ready for conflict – race of the conquering march! Race of passion and the storm."

Confederate Cavalryman

And now with slow tap to the drag
of aged feet, the steady drum
Sounds where a cross street cleaves the crag,
And down the park the old troops come.
These ancient remnants tottering by
Were comrades to a host of boys,
Brave young battalions thrown to die,
Now white like those new-budded joys.
–John Macy, "The White Brigade"

A Confederate cavalryman who served under Major-General J.E.B. Stuart is pictured in the early 1900s, some forty years after the Civil War.

The South's cavalry was made up of mostly farmers who had grown up riding horses. Despite being under-equipped – more than half their weapons were taken from Union soldiers during raids or on the battlefield – they were vastly superior.

Napoleon III toured the United States during the Civil War and one of his aides remarked, "Nothing is as picturesque as the Southern cavalry. They wear…mostly rags, hats without bottoms, boots without soles. Yet they could make Don Bazan jealous of their martial bearing and countenance."

J.E.B. Stuart was as daring as he was flamboyant. He led his cavalrymen into such key battles as 2nd Bull Run, Antietam, Fredericksburg, Chancellorsville, Gettysburg, and the Wilderness. He thundered into battle in full uniform, with a black ostrich plume in his hat, a yellow silk sash across his chest, and his personal banjo player at his side. He died in 1864 of wounds suffered in battle.

America had a special love for veterans from both sides of the Civil War. Just as the war itself tore the nation, the years after it reunited the former foes in what author Stephen Crane called a "mysterious fraternity." The 500,000 Confederate veterans were hailed as martyrs, just as the 1.5 million Union veterans were honored as heroes.

Fraternal organizations for veterans from both sides sprang up soon after the war's end. These kept friendships alive and provided for crippled veterans and for the widows and children of comrades. The most famous of these were the Grand Army of the Republic and the United Confederate Veterans.

These organizations were instrumental in establishing "homes" for the old soldiers. Said one benefactor of a Confederate home: "It is a comfort to the old veterans that a haven is provided to which they may retire and lose none of their self-respect."

Memorial Day began three years after the war, and every year the blue and gray marched in parades. Soon, almost every town, city and battlefield had a monument to these men.

Reunions brought thousands of veterans, as well as major political figures. Veterans wore their old uniforms and re-enacted old charges, meeting their former foes with an embrace. In 1913, 57,000 veterans convened in Gettysburg to mark the 50th anniversary of the battle.

"Once again does this field tremble under the tread of a mighty host – not now in fear, but in joy," declared Secretary of War Lindley M. Garrison. "This meeting is the final demonstration that the last embers of former times have been stamped out. History knows no parallel."

Of those 57,000, 2,000 returned to Gettysburg in 1938 to see Franklin D. Roosevelt dedicate the Eternal Light Peace Memorial on the seventy-fifth anniversary. Soon they, too, were gone. The last Union soldier died in 1956; the last Confederate, in 1959.

A Difficult Passage

None can realize the horrors of war, save those actually engaged.
They have paid the last penalty. They have fought their last battle.
—Soldier of the 6th Georgia

Two coachmen set out on a long journey in severe winter weather. One is driving the team of horses while the other deflects snow and wind with a large umbrella. Burials at this time were often up to 35 miles from the funeral home. The coachmen left home at five in the morning and returned home the same day, not until 10 PM or later. This meant up to seventeen hours of travel in one day.

Sitting high on the hammercloth (cloth that covered the coach box) dressed in formal attire, they had only a blanket for warmth. Every coach was equipped with a black box known as the boot, which often contained tools in case of a breakdown. The space we now call a trunk in a car is still referred to as a boot in England and Australia.

Road travel in 1900 was difficult, especially in poor weather conditions over long, hilly distances. The ordinary road required a team of four horses, and a team of six was often needed for rough, hilly roads. It was difficult to maintain smooth road surfaces. Small stones sunk down into the earth, leaving the larger stones for a carriage to bump over.

A man named John McAdam came up with a creative solution to this problem. He "macadamized" road beds with stones of equal size, paving a smoother path (in the limited number of roads that he built). In the winter, the best one could hope for was that the road had been "rolled" by large snow rollers to compact the snow.

The hearse in the painting was built in 1890 and used until 1920. It was one of the last of its type to be produced before the advent of the motorized hearse in 1909. Prior to the Civil War, hearses were utilitarian and simply built, with just a shaft for one horse. By 1856, styles began to change, becoming gradually more ornate. After that, styles changed roughly every fifteen years.

This gilded coach had shaped doors and glass panels, carved urns on top, extensive brass trim, heavy wood frame construction, and wrought iron. This made it extremely heavy, weighing in at between five and six tons.

Because of the weight, the horses had difficulty not only pulling it up hills but also in avoiding getting run over by it when traveling down hills. Drivers operated brakes on the back wheel, or simply used an iron skid, or drag-shoe, attached to a chain. This was placed under a hind wheel while going down. The hearse stopped at the top of a hill to "skid up" and again at the bottom to "skid down." Horses were also fitted with steel shoes studded with sharp caulks to improve their traction.

Coach wheels were usually made of hickory or oak spokes, elm and brass for hubs and iron for rims. The running gear was often constructed of strong, springy wood such as oak, ash, or hickory. In the early days a country blacksmith could build a decent wagon, but eventually wainwrighting or coachmaking became full-time occupations.

There are 45 stars on the flag pictured here. Utah was the most recent addition to the Union in 1896.

Boots and Saddle

In the long history of the world, only a few generations have been granted the role of defending freedom in its hour of maximum danger. I do not shrink from this responsibility, I welcome it.
–John F. Kennedy, inaugural address; inscribed on wall near his grave

Boots reversed in the stirrups accompanied by a reversed sword is one of the most striking images of a military funeral. It is a symbol that a soldier has died and will never ride again in life. This honor is traditionally only performed for Army generals, commissioned officers who served in a mounted unit, presidents, and those designated by the president.

The boots, saddle and sword are all black, except for a gold border on the saddle blanket and brass handle on the curved cavalry sword. The sword can also be thrust through the saddle blanket. The horse is black and is usually caparisoned, or hooded. An ornamental mourning covering on the horse's harness and saddle is also sometimes used.

The rider-less horse ritual probably began during the feudal wars around the time of Genghis Khan. It was believed that the horse's spirit would continue to serve the cavalryman in the next life. The custom has been popular at least since the Napoleanic wars in the early 1800s.

For example, the Duke of Wellington had what was called "the most splendid funeral ever staged in Europe." His rider-less horse was featured prominently, along with an enormous car formed from cannon captured by his army. It took a hundred men in six foundries to shape it.

When Buffalo Bill died in 1917, 25,000 people came to pay their respects and his horse McKinley followed the hearse, rider-less.

By far, the most famous of these horses is "Blackjack," the 17-year-old charger that followed President Kennedy's caisson in November of 1963. Blackjack was used for many funerals in Arlington Cemetery during his lifetime and he can be seen in many photos of military funerals held there during the 1960s.

The Third Infantry Regiment, known as the "Old Guard," trains and provides horses for state and military funerals. One of the oldest and most honored of any military unit, the Third is also responsible for guarding the Tomb of the Unknown Soldier.

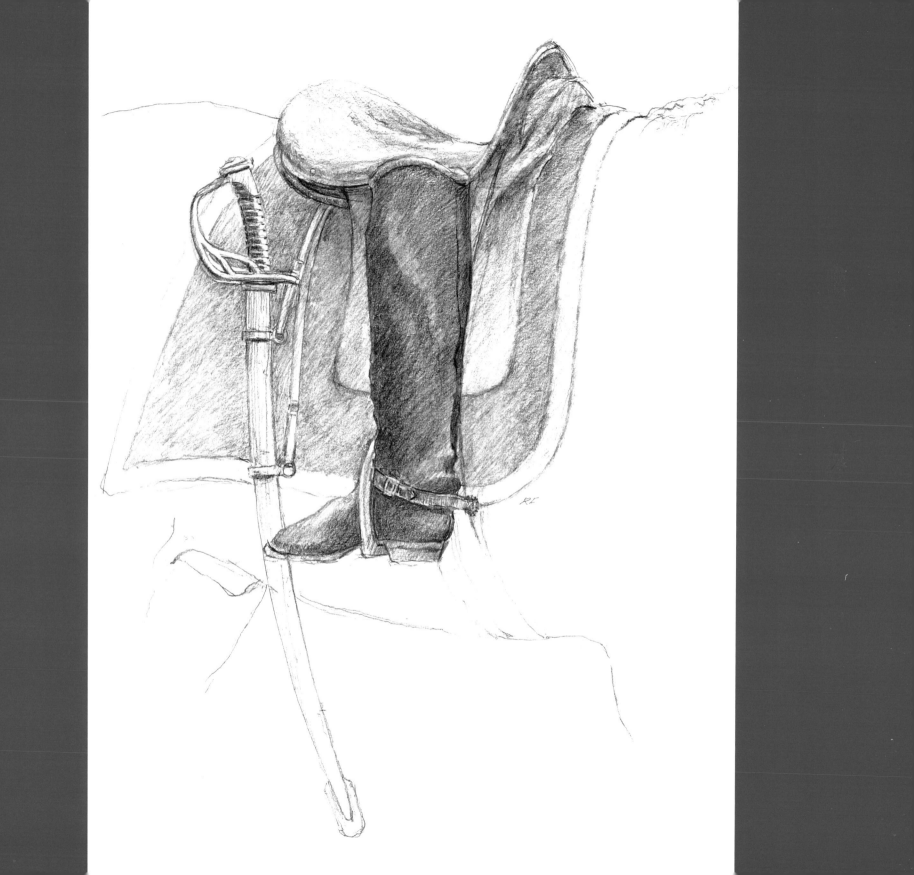

Quiet Waiting

Cold in the earth – and the deep snow piled above thee,
Far, far removed, cold in the dreary grave!
When the days of golden dreams had perished,
And even Despair was powerless to destroy,
Then did I learn how existence could be cherished,
Strengthened, and fed without the aid of joy.
Then did I check the tears of useless passion—
Weaned my young soul from yearning after thine;
Sternly denied its burning wish to hasten
Down to that tomb already more than mine.

—Emily Bronte, "Remembrance"

A fresh snow falls as the body of a Civil War veteran is carried to the waiting hearse at the New Milford United Methodist Church in New York State. All men have removed their hats out of respect for the deceased and the flag. A single horse sled has just passed, leaving the first tracks in the new snow.

A military funeral service at the time was very similar to one today: there were prayers, Bible readings, hymn singing, eulogies amd military rituals.

The street is lined with Northern Sugar Maple trees. Local residents still tap the trees in the area to make maple syrup in the early spring. The hamlet of New Milford was also known as Jockey Hollow. In 1782, Washington and his troops made a large encampment in this area en route to Washington's headquarters in Newburgh, New York. They found New Milford, "as fair as the garden of the Lord, to that famished, ragged, American hoard."

At that time, New Milford had ample resources – a grist mill, feed mill, saw mill, cider mill, distillery, orchards, streams full of fish, and forests full of game. Washington was entertained nearby at the Sanford stone house, while his officers had their headquarters near the Washington Elm, a graceful elm tree named in honor of the great general.

The Continental cavalry, once they realized they would be stationed in New Milford for a while, laid out a horse racing course along the flats just west of where the church now stands. Nearby farmers brought horses to trade and race with the soldiers, and the name Jockey Hollow was born.

In Puritan New England and New York State, the church, or meetinghouse, was one of the first buildings built in a new community. Church attendance in the early days was compulsory. Lack of attendance was punished by the secular arm of the law. The only excuse was extreme illness.

On a winter day such as is pictured, the interior of the church was as cold as the outside. Stoves in churches were opposed as a concession to carnality, and most people sat in the pews with only foot warmers containing coals from their fireplaces to keep them warm.

The meetinghouse served many functions besides the sacred. It was often town hall and civic auditorium where all town meetings and elections were held.

Driving the Procession

War, at the best, is terrible, and this war of ours, in its magnitude and in its duration,
is one of the most terrible. It has carried mourning to almost every home, until it can almost be said
that the "heavens are hung in black."

–Abraham Lincoln

Horse-drawn carriages form a slow, mournful procession to a village cemetery in New England. The horses are not blanketed because of the distance they must travel, pulling hard in the snow. Most of the coachmen are protected from the elements by canopies and woolen blankets.

The carriage in the foreground seats four to six people with the driver sitting to the right. The completely enclosed carriages are the warmest. The reins are fed through a slot, making the entire carriage almost air-tight.

The driver is holding the reins American-style (English-style is left handed). Near-side reins are held in the left and off-side reins are held in the right. If the driver is controlling a team of horses, the order of the reins is thumb and forefinger – leaders, first and middle – swing horses, and middle and ring – wheel horses.

To change direction, the horses are "chopped" which means that the reins on the turning side are all pulled together. Some drivers were famous for their expertise and could turn a galloping team 180° around in a street. Poor driving could break a pole or throw the wheel horses off their feet.

The harnesses of the horses were remarkable. Traces ran along the length of the body and were attached to the hames, a sturdy piece of wood or metal fitted on a padded neck collar. This was supported by a saddle and breaching around the horses' buttocks, which helped with stability when going down a hill.

Reins were fed through a terret (a metal loop) attached to the hames, and were attached to the bit, which ran through the horse's mouth. Most horses also wore blinders to prevent them from getting spooked at things along the roadside.

When the carriages were not in use, they were stored in a carriage house. A small door with two latches was placed over the slot to keep field mice from making a home in the padded leather horse-hair seats and wool blankets. The interiors of these carriages were heavily varnished natural wood and lavender drapes. To this day, carriages of this type in museums still smell of fresh straw and varnish.

The scene in the painting is representative of New England at that time. The six states of New England were composed of a series of villages, farmland, and woodland. Each village was a self-sufficient community with a meetinghouse, schoolhouse, taverns, stores, gristmills, sawmills, blacksmiths, millers, and general stores.

The houses were usually made of wood; it was rare to find a brick or a stone house. The leaders of the community were ministers, wealthy merchants and landowners, attorneys, and justices of the peace. Everyone else appeared somewhere on a rigid social scale. The only place where all classes mixed was the meetinghouse.

New England is rivaled perhaps only by the South in having a unique identity that is fiercely loved by its inhabitants. Thomas Hutchinson, last royal governor of the province of Massachusetts Bay, summed up this attitude when he wrote in exile, "When I die you will find engraved upon my heart 'New England'."

CHAPTER FOUR: THE SMALL WARS— SPANISH-AMERICAN AND MEXICAN WARS

I have seen soldiers die —I have been among them, may I say, of them—
and I know it is not a fearful thing to fall on a field of glorious valor among the brave, though
torn with the bolts of battle, and see the old flag go steadily on amidst the reeling lines...
Manhood asks no better death bed than that, nor is there any nearer Heaven.

—General Joshua Lawrence Chamberlain

SPANISH–AMERICAN WAR 1898   MEXICAN WAR 1846-1848

The United States was engaged in a series of "small wars" throughout the 1800s. These included the Mexican War, the Spanish-American War, and the Indian Wars. At the turn of the century, the United States helped to quell the Boxer Rebellion in China as well as insurrections in the Philippines.

The Mexican War (1846-1848), called by Ulysses S. Grant "the most unjust war," was fought both to protect the rights of Texans, the newest citizens of the United States and to fulfill the nation's self-professed "Manifest Destiny." Manifest Destiny was the idea that North America was the United States and it was the right of its citizens "to overspread the continent allotted by Providence for the free development of our yearly multiplying millions," as one magazine editor wrote.

The war was fought mainly by and for Westerners, but the result of the peace treaty signed on February 2, 1848 was that the U.S. gained 1,200,000 square miles from "sea to shining sea." The U.S. paid $15 million in what is known as the Mexican Cession.

"Remember the Alamo," was the most famous slogan to come out of the war. The slogan refers to the overtaking of the Alamo in San Antonio by Mexican general Santa Anna. All of the Alamo's defenders were killed after a 13-day siege that ended with Americans clubbing their foes with rifles due to their lack of ammunition.

Fire Fight

Mexico had a larger military but thanks to General Winfield Scott's inventive and strong leadership, the U.S. Army was soon to be known as a force to be feared in the world.

The Spanish-American War (April-August 1898) established Cuba as a power independent of Spain, the United States as a world power, and Guam, Puerto Rico, and the Philippine Islands as part of the U.S.

"Remember the Maine!" became the war's rallying cry when on February 15, 1898 the battleship Maine exploded in Havana Harbor, killing the 266 people on board.

An inquiry at the time indicated that the explosion was caused by a mine, but historians today believe that the explosion was the result of an accident on board. On June 22, 16,000 American soldiers landed on the beach in Cuba, staging the first ever overseas landing against a European power.

Col. Teddy Roosevelt and his Rough Riders emerged as heroes after their battle on Kettle Hill. In his farewell address to his troops, the future president said, "The world will be kind to you for ten days, everything you do will be all right. After that you will be judged by a stricter code, and if you prove worthless, you will be considered as spoiled by going to war."

It was also one of the first times after the Civil War that white and black soldiers fought together. Future general John J. Pershing wrote, "White regiments, black regiments fought shoulder to shoulder, unmindful of race or color, and mindful only of their common duty as Americans."

The Home Visitors

The bustle in a house
The morning after death
Is solemnest of industries
Enacted upon earth,
The sweeping up the heart,
And putting love away
We shall not want to use again
Until eternity.
−Emily Dickinson

A community gathers in 1940 at a farmhouse for the wake of a Spanish-American War veteran. Wakes and funerals were still mainly held in homes. Even though the first funeral home appeared in 1903, it wasn't until later in the 1940s in the cities that funeral homes began to be widely used. Funerals are sometimes held at home to this day; Jacqueline Onassis Kennedy's viewing was held at home.

Wakes come from an ancient custom of keeping watch over the dead in hopes that life will return. Small lavender and white flowers wrapped in a lavender ribbon were posted as a funeral badge on the door just above the door knob. The doorbell was muffled with a black ribbon.

Rose-tinted, open-top lamps were placed on either side of the casket to give more flesh tones to the deceased during viewing. Red candles were used if electricity wasn't available. Shades were often drawn for seclusion, but some houses opted to have a large window installed in the parlor facing the road so that neighbors could pay their respects without disturbing the grieving family. This is where bay windows originated and were also used for viewing a family wedding.

Undertakers usually came to the home in pairs, a male and a female, carrying a lying-in-state kit. This kit contained a kneeling board, religious icons, red candles or cellophane for lamps, and even a small organ.

The male undertaker washed the body and fumigated the house. The fumigator consisted of a stout copper ball of half-gallon capacity, with a funnel-shaped tube inserted in the keyhole of a room to be sanitized. Formaldehyde, arsenic, or zinc oxide was used.

The female assistant set up the parlor, put up the lamps, draped black fabric over portraits, placed a black wreath on the door, stopped the clocks, and covered mirrors. It was not uncommon for her to drape the parlor or sometimes the whole downstairs of the house in black or gray. She also attended to the needs of the widow, in some cases sewing her mourning dress. The thinking was that a widow would allow herself to be more emotional with another woman.

Ice was placed under the casket to keep the body cool. During the summer or for a wake lasting several days, such as an Irish wake, lace material was placed over the deceased. This partially obscured the body and kept insects away.

The funeral service itself was often deeply emotional. Author Lewis Atherton says, "While the bereaved family would not have had things otherwise, they were in for a rough hour. A long eulogy by the preacher and doleful hymns by a quartet only served to weaken those closest to the deceased and to leave them defenseless for the final ordeal at the grave."

The twentieth century saw the funerals of the last veterans of all American wars during the 1800s. Frederick Fraske, the last veteran of the Indian Wars, died in 1973 at age 101. Owen Thomas Edgar was the final veteran of the Mexican War; he died in 1929 at age 98. Nathan E. Cooke died in 1992 at age 106, the last veteran of the Spanish-American War.

CHAPTER FIVE: WORLD WAR I

In Flanders fields the poppies blow
Between the crosses, row on row,
That mark our place; and in the sky
The larks, still bravely singing, fly
Scarce heard amid the guns below.

We are the Dead.
Short days ago
We lived, felt dawn, saw sunset glow,
Loved and were loved, and now we lie
In Flanders fields.

Take up our quarrel with the foe:
To you from failing hands we throw
The torch; be yours to hold it high.
If ye break faith with us who die
We shall not sleep, though poppies grow,
In Flanders fields.

–John McCrae, "In Flanders Field"

WORLD WAR I 1914-1918

World War I took the lives of ten million soldiers and is second only to World War II in number of countries involved and sheer destruction. By the war's end, more than twenty countries had joined the Allied side.

Although the war had raged since 1914, America didn't enter until mid-June, 1917. Again woefully unprepared for a war, America had a tiny army of 200,000 men, out of a population of 100 million. By the end, however, U.S. Forces totaled five million men and women, three million of whom were drafted.

The destruction and loss of life in World War I was unprecedented. Almost ten million soldiers died on the battlefield; 21 million men were wounded. It is possible that as many civilians as soldiers died of disease and starvation. At one point, England lost 60,000 men in a day. The total cost for the war was approximately $337 billion, about $10 million an hour by 1918.

Some of the notable expressions to come out of the war were: "cooties," or head lice – 90 percent of soldiers in the trenches had them; "over the top!" (which meant go over the top of the trenches and attack) and "no man's land" (the dangerous, forlorn place between enemy lines). World War I was the first war to make massive use of mechanical innovations such as the airplane, submarine, machine gun and tank, as well as new weapons such as poison gas and flame throwers.

Poppies

Bringing the News

My message today was a message of death for our young men.
– President Woodrow Wilson, with tears in his eyes, after signing the declaration of war on April 6, 1917

A driver and his rockaway coach stop in the early evening in front of a rural, Northern general store/post office, bringing news that the United States has entered "the Great War."

In 1917, the rural general store and post office was (and still is in many places) the social hub of the village. Neighbors met every day to catch up on the latest news and pick up their mail and supplies.

On April 2, 1917, President Woodrow Wilson asked Congress to declare a state of war with Germany, using those now famous words, "The world must be made safe for democracy. Its peace must be planted upon the tested foundations of political liberty. We have no selfish ends to serve. We desire no conquest, no dominion. We seek no indemnities for ourselves, no material compensation for the sacrifices we shall freely make. We are but one of the champions of the rights of mankind. We shall be satisfied when those rights have been made as secure as the faith and the freedom of nations can make them."

Four days later, on April 6, Congress approved and the president signed the Declaration of War. Wilson had been re-elected as the "Peace President," but he was the first to lead the American people into a global war of unprecedented proportions.

Once the war was begun, a massive public relations campaign was put into place to unite a nation still deeply divided over the war. The Uncle Sam poster with the pointing finger was part of this campaign, as was a woman saying, "Gee, I wish I were a man…"

War bonds were enormously successful. Half the nation's adult population subscribed to the Fourth Liberty Loan in 1918.

The draft register was called an Honor List, which helped its image immensely. The last time there had been a draft was the Civil War, and that had resulted in bloody riots and over 100 draft officials murdered.

The government seized control of food, fuel and the railways. People who opposed the war could be brought to trial under war-time law which forbade any statement that might harm the war effort.

Popular songs at the time had titles like, "When the Kaiser Does the Goose-step to a Good Old American Rag" and "If He Can Fight Like He Can Love, Good Night, Germany." Perhaps the most popular and enduring was George M. Cohan's "Over There."

President Wilson, in his war speech, had a sense of the enormity of the coming battle. "It is a fearful thing to lead this great peaceful people into war," he said, "into the most terrible and disastrous of all wars, civilization itself seeming to be in the balance. But the right is more precious than peace, and we shall fight for the things which we have always carried nearest our hearts."

A Flyer Marries

Let us stand today in remembrance
of our own love's beginning.
Let us wave and cheer as the new bird
feels the power of muscle,
the expanse of feather
as it begins to fly.
–Rufus Collinson, "The Beginning of a Difference"

A flyer and his bride enter into the luminous sunshine of an August afternoon after a passing rain shower. The Baptist church, built in 1810 in the style of the famous English architect Christopher Wren, stands on a grassy knoll above the center of the village.

World War I marked the first time that planes were used for combat purposes. In 1914, pilots began shooting at other planes with pistols, and dropping bricks, darts and hand grenades on targets. Cockpits were too small for parachutes, and a pilot either landed safely or he died. Airmen sat on cast-iron stove lids to protect themselves from ground troops' bullets that ripped through the plane's flimsy canvas.

The finest airplane designer of the war, Anthony Fokker, created nearly sixty types of aircraft for the Germans, as well as a machine gun that fired through the airplane's prop.

Aerial warfare captured the imagination and lifted the morale of the public. Aerial "dog fights" were described as waltzes in the sky. One artilleryman watching from below said: "It's the biggest show I ever witnessed." Stories of "aces" – pilots who had downed at least five enemy planes – dominated the news. In World War I, 550 British pilots, 160 Frenchmen and 120 Americans were designated aces.

Aviation was 14 years old when the United States entered the war. American pilots, flying British and French planes, shot down 927 German airplanes and balloons while the Germans destroyed only 316.

American ace Eddie Rickenbacker downed 22 enemy planes and four German observation balloons in six months. He describes downing his first plane in his book *Fighting the Flying Circus:* "At 150 yards I pressed my triggers. The tracer bullets cut a streak of living fire into the rear of the Pfalz tail…The swerving of the Pfalz' course indicated that its rudder no longer was held by a directing hand…Curving slightly to the left the Pfalz circled a little to the south and the next minute crashed onto the ground…I had brought down my first enemy aeroplane and had not been subjected to a single shot!"

Germany's ace was Baron Manfred von Richthofen, known as the Red Baron for the crimson color of his Albatros biplane. He had the highest score of any pilot in the war, destroying 80 Allied aircraft.

The Air Force was finally recognized as a distinct service force in 1947; until then it was part of the Army. The Navy still has its air arm. Although only decades old, the Air Force is ingrained in the American psyche with images of Kitty Hawk, Chuck Yeager breaking the sound barrier, and Air Force One.

The Air Force is responsible for identifying Murphy's Law and the Global Positioning System. Modern warfare depends on the men and women who live the words of the Air Force anthem, "We live in fame or go down in flame."

General Billy Mitchell, commander of American air forces who was court-martialed for his outspoken advocacy of an independent air force, said in 1925: "It is probable that future wars again will be conducted by a special class, the air force, as it was by the armored knights of the Middle Ages."

After The Benediction

They shall not grow old, as we that are left grow old:
Age shall not weary them, nor the years condemn
At the going down of the sun and in the morning
We will remember them.

–Laurence Binyon, "For the Fallen"

Guided by two pallbearers, an honor escort dressed with white leggings and black armbands carry the casket of a fellow soldier down the stairway of the church. The pastor has just delivered the benediction and is standing at the top of the stairs with hat in hand. The dogwoods at the side of the stone church are in full bloom.

The casket is carried feet first, with the blue field and 48 stars of the flag over the heart of the deceased. An officer in charge stands in the place of honor to the right (the viewer's left) of the pallbearers. His service cap has a light brown braid around the sides, indicating that he is an officer. He wears a Sam Browne leather belt across his chest, a regulation for all officers of every allied country in Europe.

Pallbearers are dressed in white canvas leggings and wear black armbands on the left arm. Felt Montana peak campaign hats with light blue cord identify them as infantrymen. These beloved campaign hats were exchanged for wool "overseas caps" when new recruits reached Europe because there was no way to carry the felt hats in a pack. Many were cut up to make slippers for the wounded.

The pallbearers march in reverse order of their ranks, with the lowest ranking soldier in the front, signifying the triumph of death over life.

The custom of draping a casket with the national flag dates back to the Napoleonic Wars (1706-1815). The dead were carried off the field of battle on a caisson that was used mainly for transporting cannon and ammunition. The use of flags originated from the need to cover the dead on the battle zone until a casket could be built or the body buried in a field grave.

Army Major George Cocheu is responsible for most of today's military funeral customs. As a member of an honor guard during the Spanish-American War, he was horrified to see that the flags that had accompanied bodies all the way back from the Philippines were taken away before the funeral. In 1918, he recommended that a firing squad be provided for each military funeral, that a soldier of at least the same rank as the deceased accompany the body, the flag be left on the coffin and finally given to the next of kin.

Today, the flag is removed just before the casket is placed in the grave, folded and presented to a close relative. If no relative is present, the flag is given to a fellow service member or veteran.

Leaving the Prayer Meeting

Though like the wanderer, The sun gone down, Darkness be over me, My rest a stone,
Yet in my dreams I'd be nearer, my God, to thee, nearer to thee.

−Sarah F. Adams, **Nearer My God to Thee**, last words of assassinated President McKinley,
played at his funeral, at the funeral of assassinated President James Garfield, and by the orchestra of the *Titanic* as it sank.

A community leaves church after a wartime prayer service. As part of the war effort, people gathered to pray together, to get war news and to connect as a community. Churches had served this purpose throughout America since the Puritans arrived. Most New England meetinghouses still stand. Although all follow a similar pattern, each is unique and reflects the community's story.

These meetinghouses were simple structures; a conscious turning away from the ornate style of the cathedrals of Europe. They had stark interiors, clear windows, two-story facades, and blunt belfries on the center of the roof. The community was intimately involved in the design and building of their church. One New Englander said that his community's church had been built, "by our own vote, framed by our own hammers and saws, and by our own hands set in the convenientest place for us all."

In the early days, the buildings were plain, unpainted, and doubled as forts against Indian attacks. These meetinghouses were built with hand-hewn oak timbers and spruce or fir siding. The oldest frame church in America still standing is the Old Ship Meeting House in Hingham, Massachusetts, built in 1681.

Later, churches were painted white, first outside then in, and fronts became columned or pilastered. The belfry moved to the front and became a bell tower with moldings and high, graceful spires. The church was in the center of a hamlet or town in New England and at a crossroads in the South and whenever possible on the highest site available. This was for both accessibility and symbolism. It was important to most people that the first and most prominent vision of their town was the church steeple.

Bob sleighs were simple farm wagons (the pick ups or station wagons of their day) converted into sleds, making winter hauling possible. This was done by simply attaching the body of the wagon to "bobs" or runners, made of bent wood or steel.

The other style was a "cutter," or the "one-horse open sleigh," made popular by the Christmas carol. Cutters were made for winter use, with the best having bodies built along the same lines as carriages. The first one in America was known as the Landau Sleigh. Heavy and about 50 inches wide, it had a folding top, lamps, Moroccan leather upholstery and a purple body.

During that time, everyone had a sleigh and used it. One diary from New York City in the 1800s reported 40 consecutive days of sleighing. People dressed warmly in their finest: plumed hats, beaded mantles, embroidered wool, bear fur coats, beaver pelts and robes.

Turn of the century pictures show Saturday morning sleigh traffic jams on Main Streets. One reason for the traffic was that on Saturdays, rural folks brought their eggs to town to trade for groceries.

The White Carnation

Give me your tired, your poor,
Your huddled masses yearning to breathe free,
The wretched refuse of your teeming shore.
Send these, the homeless, tempest-tost to me,
I lift my lamp beside the golden door.
–Emma Lazarus, inscribed on the pedestal of the Statue of Liberty

A young widow places a white carnation on her husband's casket, while the parents and children of the deceased veteran look on. The family emigrated from Germany during the 1800s to homestead on the great plains of Kansas. The loss of a son on a small family farm was incalculable.

Adults wore black mourning dress while children wore dark blue, brown or maroon colors; girls' dresses were trimmed in black. The women in the family usually made the clothing. An army field sergeant from the deceased veteran's unit stands at attention. A 1914 Ford model T hearse, also used as an ambulance, bore the casket to the cemetery.

America is truly a nation of immigrants. "These States are the amplest poem," Walt Whitman wrote, "here is not merely a nation but a teeming Nation of nations."

Over the last two hundred years, there has been a steady flow, often broken down into "waves" by historians – "old" immigrants from the British Isles and northwestern Europe before the 1880s – and "new" immigrants after that from southern and eastern Europe. This flow has repeatedly shaped our national history. More than four million immigrants entered the United States in thirty years before the Civil War.

These millions laid the rails, built the mills and grew the food in the newly opened prairie. There were more than 500,000 immigrant volunteers in the Union Army. Free public education came about mainly as a means to quickly assimilate the children of millions of immigrants who otherwise would have continued to speak their parents' language.

The majority of immigrants have been the poor of their country. It took extraordinary will and courage to make the long, difficult passage to America's shores and beyond into the prairie.

Most colonial Germans were farmers who found a fertile area and stayed there. They built a way of life, working their land with great care, introducing crop rotation and selective cutting in their forests. This was remarkable in a time when most people were exploiting land, draining it of all potential, then moving on farther into the seemingly limitless West.

By the turn of the century, German Americans had 672,000 farms covering over a hundred million acres. World War I proved a great challenge for them. Many left in 1914 to fight for their country, long before World War I had entered into the daily consciousness of Americans.

When the United States did enter the war in 1917, many immigrants were victims of an anti-German hysteria that swept the nation, which included such silly measures as trying to rename sauerkraut "liberty cabbage."

The settling of America continues. Even today, twice as many people every year immigrate to America than are born here.

Israel Zangwill, son of poor Russian immigrants, wrote in his play, *The Melting Pot:* "America is God's crucible, the Great Melting Pot, where all races of Europe are reforming. Germans and Frenchmen, Irishmen and Englishmen, Jews and Russians, into the crucible with you all. God is making the American."

Nurse Home On Leave

I am not accustomed to the use of language of eulogy; I have never studied the art of paying compliments to women; but I must say, that if all that has been said by orators and poets since the creation of the world in praise of women were applied to the women of America, it would not do them justice for their conduct during this war. I will close by saying, God bless the women of America.

−Abraham Lincoln, speech, 1864

A nurse on leave returns to her hometown for Christmas. The railroad station at that time was a busy, vibrant place. A hotel for travelers is across the street from the station, and a baggage handler is pulling a cart to the baggage car to receive shipping, packages, and mail.

Almost every town and city in the United States had a railroad passing through it. It was a great status symbol and towns competed bitterly to entice a railroad to come through. World War I was the high point for railroads in the United States with 270,000 miles of track. Travel by horse was too slow. There were no passenger planes. Automobiles were expensive, unreliable, and the quality of the roads was inconsistent.

The automobile eventually took its toll on the railroad industry, just as it did the horse-drawn carriage. There are currently only 130,000 miles of tracks left. However, railroads today are economically stronger than any time since World War II.

Nurses have been an integral part of America's wars since George Washington requested "female nurses to attend the sick" in 1775. Six thousand nurses served in the Union army during the Civil War. One of the most famous nurses to come out of this war was Louisa May Alcott. She records a discharged patient's attitude toward nurses in her book *Hospital Sketches*: "We're off, ma'am, and I'm powerful sorry, for I'd no idea a 'orspittle was such a jolly place. Hope I'll get another ball somewheres easy, so I'll come back, and be took care of again."

Clara Barton provided the first act of war relief during the Civil War, nursing the wounded on the battlefield, establishing a supply train of food and medical supplies to the front lines, and tracing missing soldiers and marking the graves of the 13,000 Union prisoners of war who died in Andersonville Prison. She became the first president of the American Red Cross, and at 77 years old, she aided wounded soldiers during the Spanish-American War.

The Army Nurse Corps was officially established in 1901 and the Navy followed suit in 1908. Army nurses went to war before the Allied Expeditionary Forces in World War I. They were the first to fly the American flag in France while caring for the British Expeditionary Forces. By the end of the war, 21,480 nurses on active duty had saved tens of thousands of lives.

More than 59,000 American nurses served on every front in World War II. Their performance was remarkable. Fewer than four percent of the American soldiers who received medical care in the field died from wounds or disease.

In Korea and Vietnam, nurses worked even closer to the front lines in M*A*S*H units. During the Gulf War and Afghanistan War, women served in combat support roles as well as providing medical assistance.

Main Street

I see a sad procession,
And I hear the sound of coming full-key'd bugles,
And the channels of the city streets they're flooding,
As with voices and with tears.
—Walt Whitman, "Dirge for Two Veterans"

A funeral procession has just left the church. A unit of Michigan Wolverines follows the hearse down Main Street. Six pallbearers flank the 1922 Packard hearse, followed by an honor guard and family.

A young 1st Lieutenant, seated next to the driver, is in charge of the interment. He wears a shoulder patch identifying his fighting unit. These unit patches were authorized by General Pershing near the end of World War I. In fact, most patches weren't designed and worn until after the men had returned to the United States.

The use of a motorized hearse was a new development. Even though the first motorized coach (essentially a carriage mounted on an auto chassis) appeared in 1909, it took another 15 years for the American public to accept it. New York City was the last major city to maintain the tradition of the horse-drawn hearse.

This 1922 Packard Limousine Hearse has smooth, simple lines. The public had grown weary of ornately carved vehicles (one particularly ostentatious 1920 vehicle had a statue of Gabriel blowing his horn). The Packard's body is made of wood, the interior of gray cloth. The seat is dark brown, ribbed leather padded with horse-hair. The steering wheel is made of wood.

The soldiers are wearing a model 1917 wool tunic and wool breeches with a "choker collar" fastened with hooks and eyes. This uniform was extremely uncomfortable but remained mandatory in both field and garrison duty until 1926. Wool uniforms exacerbated the heat and horror of a static war (the Western Front hardly moved in over three years of fierce fighting) in the summer.

Captain Reginald Leetham wrote in his diary: "There were twice the number of dead men than live ones. As the day went on, it got hotter and hotter. I thought at the time I should never get rid of the peculiar disgusting smell of the vapor of warm human blood. I would rather have smelt gas a hundred times. To do one's duty one was continually climbing over corpses in every position."

Officers wore a belt with a strap over the shoulder to support the weight of a handgun. This style belt, known as a Sam Browne, was copied from the British military.

In 1928, the Corps dropped the high collar of the uniform. Between 1928 and 1954 there were numerous changes to the uniforms. These changes include the abolishment of the Sam Browne (1942 – now only worn with Blue-White dress) and the change in color of leather items from brown to black (1963). Uniforms have been basically the same since 1954.

The Michigan Wolverines trace their history back to the Civil War when Brigadier-General George Armstrong Custer, later to meet infamy at Little Big Horn, led the 1st Michigan Cavalry in a key role in the epic battle of Gettysburg in 1863.

Twenty-three-year-old Custer, four days before only a Captain, held the Federal center by leading the lone veteran regiment with the cry, "Come on, you Wolverines!"

A Veteran Dies at Home

Gas! Gas! Quick, boys! – An ecstasy of fumbling,
Fitting the clumsy helmets just in time;
But someone still was yelling out and stumbling
And flound'ring like a man in fire or lime…
Dim, through the misty panes and thick green light,
As under a green sea, I saw him drowning.
–Wilfred Owen, "Dulce Et Decorum Est"

An undertaker carries a veteran's uniform out to the hearse sled on an early winter morning. A sharpshooter has died at home from lingering effects of exposure to mustard gas in Europe.

Overall, gas casualties during World War I totaled nearly one million men. This number does not take into account the vast number of casualties from the long-term effects of gas exposure.

The Hague Convention foresaw the devastation that chemical weapons could cause. It was agreed that projectiles would not be used whose sole purpose was the diffusion of asphyxiating or deleterious gases. All attending delegates signed the resolution except the United States. When the Germans launched the first chlorine attack on April 22, 1915 at Ypres, a five-mile-wide cloud of chlorine gas from 168 tons of the chemical, the world was outraged.

The Germans justified their use of poison gas by pointing out that France used 26-mm gas grenades in August, 1914. French newspapers reported that France was developing a liquid explosive, turpinite, which gave off lethal fumes. Around this time, a French bombardment left German soldiers dead of asphyxiation, and French papers were captured that described chloroacetone cartridges, grenades, and their use. The Germans felt they had their proof that they were not the first to break the Hague Convention and were now free to use poison gas.

Regardless of how it began, the French and British soon followed Germany's lead into a deadly new form of warfare.

The gases were classified according to their actions: eye irritants or "tear gas" causing temporary blindness, nasal irritants or "vomiting gases," respiratory irritants or "suffocating gases" which were used to kill, and skin irritants. The skin irritant gases arrived later in the war but soon became the most infamous. First used on July 12, 1917, it was called 'yperite' by the French, but the British and Americans simply called it 'mustard gas' because of its similarity to mustard in both color and smell. Mustard gas worked whether soldiers wore gas masks or not by causing skin burns, even through clothing. It was toxic in concentrations that couldn't be detected by smell. Symptoms might not be evident until many hours later.

An Allied nurse said, "I wish those people who write so glibly about this being a holy war and the orators who talk so much about going on no matter how long the war lasts and what it may mean, could see a case – to say nothing of ten cases – of mustard gas in its early stages, could see the poor things burnt and blistered all over with great mustard-colored suppurating blisters, … with voices a mere whisper, saying that their throats are closing and they know they will choke."

The use of gas during World War I may have precluded its use during World War II. In 1918, Adolf Hitler, then a German corporal was blinded temporarily by a gas attack in Flanders. He developed a fear of gas and chose not to use it as a weapon during World War II.

The Major and His Wife

I saw his round mouth's crimson deepen as it fell,
Like a sun, in his last deep hour;
Watched the magnificent recession of farewell,
Clouding, half gleam, half glower,
And a last splendour burn the heavens of his cheek.
And in his eyes
The cold stars lighting, very old and bleak,
In different skies.
–Wilfred Owen

A major and his wife enter the cemetery in a rural glass-paneled undertaker's coach for the burial of one of his men. A mounted lieutenant (whose horse's head is seen on the left) directs the procession as it enters the cemetery.

Many veterans' graves can be seen, identified with flags. The major's jacket flap bars identify active duty in various European campaigns during World War I. The crossed-rifle insignia indicates the rifle company he commanded. The major's wife is dressed all in black with a full veil, and a hat of ostrich feathers.

Horses and carriages were still used for funerals until the 1930s – people thought a motorized hearse was indecent. Horses are still used in high profile funerals. However, World War I marked the final practical use of horses in the cavalry in warfare. There were a limited number of ships to transport horses to Europe and many of the ships that attempted the voyage were sunk by German U-Boats.

The demand was there, however, and America sent 357,000 horses to England and France in 1916. The numbers decreased from there, as the ships were needed to transport American troops.

The use of horses was limited in many ways by World War I. The massive demand by war-torn Europe for grain meant that all available grain needed to be shipped. This led directly to motors displacing horses in urban areas, despite the fact that the peak year for American carriage-making was a mere ten years earlier in 1905 with the manufacture of 930,000.

Motor use spread to farms, and within twenty years the draft horse had all but disappeared. Horse-drawn caissons on the battlefield were replaced by big trucks carrying many times the load of a caisson. Horses that died in action became fresh meat for the soldiers' mess.

The Army had 86,000 horses, and the sabered cavalry troops were the Army's elite. However, cavalry was not used on World War I battle lines after 1915. This fact escaped the War Department; they bought 1,000,000 horse blankets, 2,000,000 feed bags, 945,000 saddles, and 2,800,000 halters.

The buying spree was not limited to the cavalry; 20 million mosquito nets were ordered for a war that had no mosquitos. General Pershing, commander of the Allied Expeditionary Forces, finally had to tell the War Department to stop sending bathtubs, bookcases, floor wax, lawn mowers, office desks, stepladders, and spittoons.

The romantic image of the sabered cavalry did not die easily. Despite such forward thinkers as Lieutenant Colonel George S. Patton, the Army in 1921 instituted the Army Remount Breeding Plan, encouraging Americans to raise thoroughbreds. The program, which kept a standing force of 700 horses, lasted until World War II.

The Parlor

You are not here. I know that you are gone,
And will not ever enter here again.
And it seems to me, if I should speak,
Your silent step must wake across the hall;
If I should turn my head, that your sweet eyes
Would kiss me from the door.
The room is as you left it; your last touch —
A thoughtless pressure, knowing not itself
As saintly — hallows now each simple thing;
Hallows and glorifies, and glows between
The dust's gray fingers like a shielded light.
—Edna St. Vincent Millay

In the parlor a fellow veteran pays his last respects as the widow looks on. The parlor historically was a special room in the home and was never entered lightly. It was the room where guests were entertained. If the family owned a piano, it would be kept in the parlor. Women did their needlework there. On Sundays, the family read the Bible there. If a young man came courting, he might sit in the parlor under the watchful eye of the grandmother while his date played the piano for him.

Some families formalized the parlor so much that, as one writer put it, it was never opened "except for the solemnization of a marriage and the obsequies of the dead."

The best furniture was kept there; walls were usually stenciled; curtains were often fringed and colorfully stitched; and the rag carpets were colorful. Children had to wash their hands and wear their best clothing in order to enter.

The widow in the painting is wearing a maroon mourning dress with black trim. This was a change from 19th century custom. A widow then was expected to wear dull black clothing for a full year reflecting the loss of luster in life because of her deceased husband. During the first six months, she was in "deep mourning," and was prohibited from taking part in any social affairs. Her clothing and accessories were usually made of black funeral crepe, although bombazine, alpaca, silk, kid, and cotton were also used.

In the second year, the widow wore shiny black (silk or crepe de chine) for the first six months, and white or violet for the last six months. She was able to wear normal clothing after two years, although if she was widowed late in life she would often wear mourning garments for the rest of her life.

The veteran is wearing wrapped canvas puttees (leggings). Soldiers of World War I wore either spirally wrapped canvas, wool, or leather wrapped puttees, or one-piece canvas or leather leggings. Men were also issued spare boots; the two pairs were to be alternated and dry socks to be worn. This was to prevent trench foot, caused by standing in cold, wet trenches, which resulted in many casualties.

The casket is made of simple wood panels with plain brass handles. A draped and tasseled black velvet border is draped around it. Before embalming, coffins were large boxes, with a metal bottoms. Ice was placed (and continually replaced) at the bottom of the coffin and the body was placed on a "cooling board" – a board with holes in it – on the ice. This separated the body from the ice (which would have made it decompose faster) while keeping the body cool.

Apple Blossoms

When we assumed the soldier, we did not lay aside the citizen.
−George Washington, letter to Continental Congress, 1775; inscribed on Memorial Amphitheater

A veteran returns to his farm in April, 1919, five months after Armistice Day, at apple blossom time. His wife has brought the noon meal in a wicker basket; his brother plows the field; and his son collects rocks from the newly tilled earth.

Captain Oliver Wendell Holmes reflected the theme of coming home in a letter to his family during the Civil War, "Very probably we shall [fight or be killed] in a few days. I have lived on the track on which I expect to continue traveling if I get through, hoping always that though it may wind it will bring me up the hill once more with the deepest love."

Many did not return. In the first year of World War I, half of all French families received "the telegram" reporting that their loved one had died. More than one million artillery shells were fired in four hours at the Battle of St. Mihiel alone.

America's entry into the war tipped the manpower numbers in the Allies' favor. On the eleventh hour of the eleventh day of the eleventh month in 1918, Armistice (a cease fire) was declared, against General Pershing's protests. He thought that the Germans should be made to surrender.

Armistice set the seed for World War II. Since Germany had never been invaded, Germans felt they could have won and were angry at the German politicians they called the "November criminals."

Norman Collins recalls when Armistice was declared, "My first feeling was it's too late, all my friends are gone, it's too late. I had a vision, and I was standing in a trench and at eye level there were feet marching, marching feet going along, and these were all the men I had known who were killed in the war. And they were marching away into the distance where I would never follow. All the people I knew had gone. Except me."

On November eleventh, both sides, knowing that the eleventh hour was near, blazed away with every gun they had. Lieutenant Walter Davenport said, "It was 10:60 precisely, and the roar stopped like a motor car hitting a wall. The resulting quiet was uncanny."

Philip Gibbs wrote in *The New York Times,* "Last night, for the first time since August in the first year of the war, there was no light of gunfire in the sky, no sudden stabs of flame through darkness, no spreading glow above black trees where for four years of nights human beings were smashed to death. The Fires of Hell had been put out."

Occupation forces left slowly. In May, 1919, 300,000 men sailed out. By the end of August, all but five divisions regularly stationed on the Rhine had left. General Pershing sailed home in September. One returning sailor, upon entering the New York Harbor at last and seeing the Statue of Liberty said, "Old girl, if you ever want to look me in the face again, you'll have to turn around on your pedestal."

WORLD WAR II

There is a mysterious cycle in human affairs. To some generations much is given. Of other generations much is expected. This generation of Americans has a rendezvous with destiny.

–Franklin Delano Roosevelt

We shall fight on the beaches. We shall fight on the landing grounds. We shall fight in the fields, and in the streets, we shall fight in the hills. We shall never surrender. Today we may say aloud before an awe-struck world: We are still masters of our fate. We are still captains of our souls.

–Winston Churchill

WORLD WAR II 1939–1945

World War II was responsible for more deaths, more destruction of property and more pervasive change than any other war in history. It is estimated that nearly one hundred million men, women, and children died as a result of WWII. The War cost more than one trillion dollars. Over fifty countries fought on almost every continent – from the deserts of Africa to the Pacific and Atlantic Oceans; from the frozen countryside of Russia, to the streets of the cities of Europe.

Six million Jews, four million gypsies, homosexuals, mentally ill, and disabled were put to death by the Germans.

Four million Poles died as a result of persecution. Russia alone lost 20 million soldiers and civilians, more than the total war casualty of WWI for all sides. The U.S. lost roughly 500,000.

It was during World War II that an atomic bomb was first used, bringing the dawn of the Atomic Age and nuclear power. War then became mechanized , employing bombers, jet fighters, aircraft carriers, tanks, ballistic missiles and paratroopers. The result was wholesale destruction.

The war was won by the military "greatest generation" men and women united in preparation for war and their willingness to fight. America's "home front" pulled off astounding feats of production. Overall, the Allies mobilized over 60 million soldiers, while the Axis had half that number.

General Attends

The Home Front – Opening the Roads

Slowly upon the ways the gray ships rise,
The hammers ring on forepeak, hold and keel.
Under our gloved hands and hooded eyes
The blue arc stitches up the patterned steel.
Over the hulls, between the clanging cranes,
We climb and kneel and seam the ships together,
Women are always sewing for their men,
It tides the heart through many a bitter weather.
The chattering rivets button up the shell,
The waiting bay is laced with windy foam,
The molten stitches glow beneath my hand,
This is the ship on which he may come home.

–Irene Carlisle, "Welder," a poem that appeared in *The Saturday Evening Post* in February, 1945

The poster is famous: Rosie the Riveter in coveralls and red handkerchief, rolling her sleeves up and declaring, "We can do it!"

America agreed, and the "home front" produced an astounding amount of war material during World War II. Everyone helped where they could; here a 1920s-era retired school bus attached with a plow keeps the roads open for defense workers and the military.

More than six million women took jobs in every profession. A third of all aircraft workers were female, as were ten percent of shipyard and steel mill workers. One woman said, "The men may have started this war, but the women are running it."

The Women's Army Auxiliary Corps numbered 200,000 women on active duty, doing everything from repairing trucks to making aerial surveys.

Everything – fuel, meat, cigarettes, tires, liquor, laundry soap, tissues, diapers, thumbtacks – was rationed. Each month over three billion ration stamps changed hands. Horsemeat sometimes became a substitute for beef and *Gourmet Magazine* wrote, "although it isn't our usual habit, this year we're eating the Easter rabbit."

Americans purchased $135 billion in war bonds to help pay for $335 billion of government expenditures. Hollywood helped – Betty Grable's stockings were auctioned off for $40,000, and Hedy Lamarr kissed anyone who bought $25,000 worth of bonds. Singer Kate Smith sold $40 million worth in one 16-hour radiothon.

Americans planted 20 million Victory gardens in 1943 and grew one-third of all the vegetables eaten. Scrap drives by children brought in countless tons of material. The Boy Scouts alone collected 54,000 tons of rubber. By the war's end, most of the steel and tin used in production was scrap.

Auto-makers stopped building cars in 1942 and more than 200,000 businesses switched their production to military material. Employment in the aircraft industry rose from 100,000 in 1940 to two million. Travel switched almost exclusively to the railroad, which transported two million soldiers a month for a total of 43 million.

The United States produced more war material than all Axis countries combined, twice as many airplanes, and a ship a day. Even Josef Stalin proposed a toast: "To American production, without which this war would have been lost."

All of these efforts not only helped win the war but also were incredible morale boosters. People felt that they were of use and that in some way they were helping bring their loved ones back home safely.

One of the best stories to come out of the Home Front is that of a sailor named Elgin Staples. His ship sank off Guadalcanal. He was swept overboard, but was saved by a life belt. It had been inspected, packed and stamped back home in Akron, Ohio…by his own mother.

Burial at Sea

Sunset and evening star and one clear call for me!
And may there be no moaning of the bar, when I put out to sea…
Twilight and evening bell,
And after that the dark!
And may there be no sadness of farewell, when I embark;
For tho' from out our bourne of time and place the flood may bear me far,
I hope to see my Pilot face to face when I have crossed the bar.
–Alfred Lord Tennyson, "Crossing the Bar"

A burial at sea is held aboard a Coast Guard cutter in the North Atlantic. During World War II, when naval forces were out to sea for weeks or months at a time, such burials were both common and unforgettable. As Charles A. Dana said, "Death is at all times solemn but never so much as at sea."

The body is sewn in a canvas shroud or placed in a coffin and weighted to ensure sinking. According to ancient custom, the sailmaker when sewing the shroud takes the last stitch through the nose of the deceased sailor as a final check to see if he's truly dead. Herman Melville writes of this tradition in *White Jacket.*

A sea burial has two parts: the religious and military. The chaplain reads the scripture and prayers, the committal, and the benediction. Military personnel perform the rest of the service. The call goes out, "all hands bury the dead," and all sailors not on duty attend the service.

The flag covers the shroud or coffin. Six to eight pallbearers form on both sides and carry the body feet first and place it on a stand with feet overboard. The chaplain reads the burial service. After the firing party is commanded to attention and "present arms," the committal (slightly different for every religion) is read.

The casket bearers tilt the board until the body or the casket slides from under the flag into the sea. All bow their heads as the benediction is pronounced, and the firing party fires three volleys. Finally, "Taps" is played.

In the war's beginning, the North Atlantic looked much as it did during World War I. German U-Boats hunted in "wolf packs" and sunk more than 700,000 tons of shipping, despite convoys escorted by armed Coast Guard, Navy and Merchant Marine ships.

With more warships, more aircraft, and better anti-submarine devices such as the depth charge (pictured on the right in the painting), the situation changed by 1943, with more U-Boats destroyed (74) than ships sunk (58). The longest and most important battle of the war, Winston Churchill said this of the Battle of the North Atlantic: "Never for one moment could we forget that everything elsewhere depended on its outcome."

Winter duty in one of the stormiest, dreariest seas on earth was incredibly dangerous; waves at times would be more than 50 feet high and everything on deck was coated with ice. One in 26 mariners serving aboard merchant ships died in the line of duty, a greater percentage than any other service.

Many veterans and family members have chosen to be buried at sea since World War II. The most recent famous burial at sea was John F. Kennedy Jr. in 1999.

Caesar at Bougainville

Uncommon valor was a common virtue.
–Admiral Nimitz

Caesar, an 87-pound German Shepherd, brings a message to Marine Company "M" during the battle of Bougainville in the South Pacific. Rufus Mayo, one of his handlers, is removing the message pinned to Caesar's collar.

Bougainville was the largest of the Solomon Islands. On November 1, 1943, the first day of combat, radio communications were impossible in the thick jungle. Caesar completed nine runs over 31 miles under heavy fire, delivering orders, overlays, and captured Japanese documents between rifle company "M" and the 2nd Battalion Command Post, where the messages were received by Caesar's second handler, John Kleeman.

On Day Two, a sleeping Caesar heard a sound. His handler Mayo awoke at the movement of his dog in time to see a grenade dropping at their feet. The handler threw it back in the direction it had come from, where it exploded, killing eight Japanese.

On the third day, the enemy tried another sneak attack. Although he wasn't trained to attack, Caesar leaped at the Japanese soldiers. The handler called the dog back to his position. As the dog returned, he was shot twice.

One shot lodged deep behind his left shoulder, close to his heart, and the field surgeon thought it too risky to remove. Caesar returned stateside, where he recovered, and carried the bullet in him for the rest of his life. He served on war-bond tours and even received a kiss from screen beauty Hedy Lamarr.

Caesar grew up in the Bronx, purchased by three brothers who had saved their allowances. When they made trips to the grocery for their mother, they would give their purchases to Caesar to carry back unaccompanied to their fourth-floor walk-up.

The brothers enlisted Caesar for the war at the same time they did. He was part of the first official U.S. war dog platoon in history. The First Marine Dog Platoon consisted of 48 enlisted men working in pairs as handlers for the 21 Dobermans and three Shepherds. They hit the beach under heavy fire just one hour after the first Marines. The war dogs were an extraordinary success. No unit protected by one of the dogs was ever ambushed or infiltrated by the Japanese.

There were three kinds of war dogs. Messenger dogs carried messages, ammunition or special medical supplies from one handler to the other handler, avoiding all other men. Sentry dogs were trained to bark to warn fixed (often sleeping) troops of the enemy's approach. Scout dogs alerted the troops of the enemy nearby silently without barking.

War dogs have played a role in every U.S. war since World War I, when a stray bull terrier named Stubby carried messages, sought out battlefield wounded, warned of gas attacks, and attacked a German soldier while on sentry duty.

Ten thousand dogs served during World War II, all volunteered by their families. The 26th Scout Dog Platoon served in Korea, and included York, who completed 148 combat patrols. Four thousand dogs served in Vietnam. Some 30,000 dogs have served in the last 50 years. One study showed that they cut casualties by over 65 percent whenever they were on the front line.

Tom Mitchell, a Vietnam dog handler, said: "When we were sick, they would comfort us, and when we were injured, they protected us. They loved us unconditionally. And we loved them. Still do."

After the Prayers

Eternal Father, strong to save,
whose arm hath bound the restless wave,
who gives the mighty ocean deep
its own appointed vigil keep,
Oh hear us when we cry to thee
for those in peril on the sea.

−from "The Navy Hymn," written in 1860 by William Whiting. This hymn was played at the funerals of
Franklin D. Roosevelt and John F. Kennedy. Every service at the U.S. Naval Academy at Annapolis and the Navy Chapel in
Washington, D.C., closes with the first stanza.

A three-volley salute marks the passing of a World War II sailor as family and friends look on. The sun breaks through a passing August storm, lighting the colors of the 48-star flag. The firing party is made up of six sailors—the chaplain is at the foot of the casket, and the officer in charge is behind him to his right. The bugler is at the end of the line of pallbearers, preparing to play "Taps" when the salute has ended.

The three-volley salute is a military funeral custom dating back to the 14th century, when firearms began to appear on the battlefield. The Germans fired three volleys in the name of the Trinity. Firing three volleys provided a means for opposing armies to declare a truce. It allowed each side time to clear their dead from the battlefield. When the burial ceremonies were completed, the volleys were fired again, signaling that burials were over and battle would commence.

The firing party at a graveside is composed of from five to eight riflemen and follows a very strict set of regulations. The firing party, pallbearers, and bugler all take position approximately 100 feet from the head or the foot of the grave and await the arrival of the funeral procession. The officer in charge commands, "Detail! Attention! and Present arms!" as soon as the casket is moved from the hearse. After the casket is placed on the grave, the firing party is commanded, "Order arms!" by the officer in charge and is given the order, "Ceremonial at ease." The clergyman leads the committal service and after the prayers, the officer in charge signals the firing party to "Attention!"

The firing party stands at the gravesite, in position to fire directly over the grave. The officer commands, "Load!" Each rifleman executes "Port arms," faces to the half right and moves his right foot ten inches to the right. He then chambers a round, places the weapon in the safe position and resumes "Port arms."

The officer commands "Ready!" Each rifleman moves the safety to the fire position. On the command "Aim!," the rifle is shouldered with both hands at a forty-five degree angle. The trigger is squeezed on the command of "Fire!" and the weapon is returned to "Port arms." The firing party fires a total of three volleys and then the officer commands, "Cease firing!" The riflemen place their weapon on Safe, assume the position of "Attention at port arms!" "Face to half left," and then "Present arms." The bugler then sounds "Taps." The firing party is commanded to "Order arms!" while the flag is folded. The officer then commands "Right face!, Port arms, and Forward march!" The weapons are unloaded and cleared as soon as possible after leaving the graveside.

Patton's Men

If I do my full duty, the rest will take care of itself.
–General George S. Patton, Jr.

A farmer proudly wears the patch of his son's division, the 2nd Armored Division, 3rd Army. The farmer was a tanker under George S. Patton, Jr. in World War I. Now his son is serving under General Patton. It was common during World War II for the people at home to wear some reminder of their loved ones who were fighting overseas. Father and son share a deep loyalty to Patton, a bond connecting all men that served under him.

Patton grew up listening to his father read the stories of the ancient Greek heroes. Civil War hero John "Ranger" Mosby often visited the Patton home and told young George his Civil War tales.

Whatever George Patton did, he did with his entire will. At West Point, he became an expert fencer. After suffering three broken noses and two broken arms playing football, he became one of the Army's best polo players. In 1912, Patton represented the U.S. in the Olympics in the Modern Pentathlon.

In 1916, Patton accompanied General Pershing in his raids into Mexico against Pancho Villa. There he killed the leader of Villa's bodyguard and another man. He placed two notches on his trademark single-action Colt revolver.

Once the U.S. entered World War I, George accompanied Pershing to Europe. He became the first American assigned to the new Tank Corps and fought in the world's first major tank battle.

In combat, he was fearless. He was wounded severely in one battle and received a Purple Heart, a Distinguished Service Cross, and a promotion. He was severely injured at least three times and came close to death twice from embolisms.

After World War I, Patton learned to fly planes, and began to watch maneuvers from the air. Because of this technique, the Army began to use observation planes.

Patton trained his men hard, believing "an ounce of sweat will save a gallon of blood." The 2nd Armored Division stayed in the field as long as 17 weeks, and the tankers would go without sleep for 36 hours or more. He made memorable, profanity-laced speeches and earned the nickname "Old Blood and Guts." Even today 3rd Army veterans proudly say they served under Patton, and all remember his words: "Now I want you to remember that no bastard ever won a war by dying for his country. You win it by making the other poor dumb bastard die for his country."

Wherever they fought, Patton's men attained incredible successes. They pushed the Germans out of North Africa, and then took Sicily. They swept through northern France, covering 600 miles in two weeks.

When they were needed the most, in the Battle of the Bulge, Patton's men made a record-breaking march in two days through extreme weather. The 3rd Army drove into Germany, squeezed off the German "bulge," saved Bastogne, and took 100,000 German prisoners. By the end of the war, the 3rd Army had inflicted almost 1.5 million casualties on the enemy and liberated 82,000 square miles of territory.

A few days before his death, Patton wrote: "Anyone in any walk of life who is content with mediocrity is untrue to himself and to American tradition." This spirit has caused many to call Patton the greatest military commander in U.S. history.

The Platoon

The generation that carried on the war has been set apart by its experience. Through our great good fortune, in our youth our hearts were touched with fire. It was given to us to learn at the outset that life is a profound and passionate thing.

–Oliver Wendell Holmes, Jr.

Seven honorary pall-bearers led by one officer accompany a flag-draped casket to the front of a city cathedral. They are all that remain of an infantry platoon who served in Europe during World War II.

Roughly 16 million World War II veterans are alive today. The Veterans Administration estimates that 574,000 veterans died in 2000, with 66 percent from World War II. This number is expected to grow to a peak of 620,000 in 2008.

The Veterans of Foreign Wars and the American Legion help keep the memories and bonds of these men alive. In war time, strangers become linked forever in an indescribable bond. They share memories of training, travel, survival during winter, summer, sickness, frost, mud, seeing friends killed and killing the enemy.

Louis Simpson, poet and WW II veteran writes, "Most clearly of that battle I remember/The tiredness of eyes, how hands looked thin/Around a cigarette, and the bright ember/Would pulse with all the life there was within."

During World War II, usually about 30 men were in a platoon, made up of four squads. Each squad contained one BAR man (who manned a Browning automatic rifle) and six riflemen.

A rifle platoon today is made of 38 men. There are two people to a fire team and two fire teams to a squad, led by a squad leader. Four squads, a platoon sergeant and a lieutenant make up a platoon. There are usually three to four platoons to a company, along with a sergeant and a captain in charge. Four companies make a battalion. A brigade is made of 3,000 soldiers, and a division, 20,000.

Oliver Wendell Holmes, Jr. spoke stirringly of the veteran's experience in one of his famous Memorial Day speeches entitled "The Soldier's Faith."

He said: "At the same time the doors opened at the front, and up the main aisle advanced his coffin, followed by the few gray heads who stood for the men of the Twentieth, the rank and file whom he had loved, and whom he led for the last time.

"The church was empty. No one remembered the old man whom we were burying, no one save those next to him, and us. And I said to myself, 'The Twentieth has shrunk to a skeleton, a ghost, a memory, a forgotten name which we other old men alone keep in our hearts.' And then I thought: 'It is right. It is as the colonel would have it.' This also is part of the soldier's faith: Having known great things, to be content with silence."

Chapter Seven: Korean War

They went not for conquest and not for gain,
but only to protect the anguished and the innocent.
They suffered greatly and by their heroism
in a thousand forgotten battles they added a
luster to the codes we hold most dear:
duty, honor, country, fidelity, bravery, integrity.
–William Sessions, former FBI director and Korean War veteran

KOREAN WAR 1950-1953

It is called "The Forgotten War," yet in many ways the Korean War was a conflict as important as World War II.

The two world superpowers, the U.S. and the Soviet Union, had moved to enforce their influence in Europe and Asia, in some cases dividing countries into Eastern and Western partitions. In Europe, Germany was divided into East and West; in Asia, it was Korea, split into North and South.

From the late nineteenth century until the end of World War II, Korea had been occupied by Japan. After the war, the United States spent four years installing a representative Republic in the South, while the Soviet Union and The People's Republic of China supported a Communist regime in the North.

In 1949, America withdrew its troops from South Korea. Within a year, on June 25, 1950, North Korea, with Chinese and Soviet support, invaded and rapidly occupied most of the southern part of the partitioned country.

The United Nations condemned the invasion and committed a 12-nation multi-national force led by the U.S. to repel it. Each side fielded armies totaling more than a million men.

The United Nations troops, commanded by Gen. Douglas MacArthur, divided the invaders with a daring landing at Inchon and drove the North Koreans all the way to the Yalu River, the border between North Korea and China. A counterattack led by 300,000 Chinese troops pushed them back into the south, where a two-year stalemate ensued.

A truce was finally brokered in 1953 after the death of Soviet dictator Josef Stalin. The war lasted three years and one month. The human toll was 580,000 Allied casualties, 116,000 of whom died, including 54,000 Americans; 1,591,000 Chinese and North Korean casualties, and an estimated one million civilian deaths in South Korea alone.

Nearly half a century later, North and South Korea still have not signed a final peace agreement.

Amazing Grace

Amazing Grace, how sweet the sound,
that saved a wretch like me.
I once was lost, but now I'm found,
was blind, but now I see.
–Hymn lyrics by John Newton, published in 1779

A lone piper, clad in traditional Highland tartan, stands next to the flag-draped coffin. He plays "Amazing Grace," a hymn that is uniquely suited to the bagpipes. The ancient instrument traditionally has led soldiers into battle as well as into the next life.

"Amazing Grace" has become a standard at funerals, both military and civilian. The story of its composition and composer is remarkable.

John Newton was born in England to a devout mother who taught him scripture and hymns at an early age. At the age of 11, he went to sea, eventually to become involved in the African slave trade. He grew to be a loud and profane man who earned the nickname, "The Great Blasphemer."

In March of 1748, at the age of 23, Newton and his ship were caught in a violent North Atlantic storm. Battered and blown for more than a week, Newton found himself desperately fighting the helm during an 11-hour watch. Exhausted and despairing, he began thinking of the scriptures his mother had taught him so many years before.

Newton and the ship survived, and he was transformed by the experience. Abandoning his former habits, he began to study the Bible. Eventually, he left the life of the sea and moved to the small English town of Olney and became a minister.

It was his habit to compose hymns for his congregation to recite during Sunday services. At the time, such works were not set to music, but were instead chanted. In 1779, William Cowper compiled and published 280 of Newton's hymns, which circulated around England and to the newly founded United States as well.

It was in America that someone put the words of the hymn Newton had called "Faith's Review and Expectation," but which already was commonly known as "Amazing Grace," to the music of an old plantation spiritual called "Loving Lambs."

Bagpipers have been associated with military units at least since Roman times. Even today, at least one American military post, Tinker Air Force Base in Oklahoma, has an official post piper. It was only natural that the pipers would pick up "Amazing Grace," whose simple, plaintive melody and message of redemption are so uniquely suited to funeral services.

It has been a comfort to millions, one of the most enduring and emotional hymns ever written.

"Taps"

Day is done. Gone the sun,
From the lake, from the hills,
From the sky. All is well,
Safely rest, God is nigh.
−from "Taps," music by General Daniel Adams Butterfield, lyrics anonymous

No bugle call is more evocative or more familiar to Americans than "Taps." Since 1891, this simple yet haunting melody has been played at every military funeral, and generations of soldiers have listened to it in camp every evening signaling "lights out." "Taps" has served as both the final call of the day and the final farewell to a human life.

Until the advent of portable electronic communications in the twentieth century, bugle calls were vital to coordinate large bodies of troops. The piercing notes of the military bugle cut through the din of an army on the march or in combat.

Officers were required not just to memorize a wide range of standard calls, which were set down in military textbooks, but also to be able to play them. In addition to the bugle calls that were universal to all military units, commanders could also devise calls for their own troops.

The man given credit for composing "Taps," Gen. Daniel Adams Butterfield, commander of a brigade of the V Corps of the Army of the Potomac during the Civil War, did not intend to create a great or lasting piece of music.

The General, recipient of a Congressional Medal of Honor for heroism, confessed to not being able to read or write music, but felt that the existing call for lights out needed to be revised. During the Peninsular Campaign in July, 1862, when the Union Army was beaten back in an attempt to take Richmond, Butterfield experimented with different tunes. His wife wrote down the notes for him.

The twenty-four-note call that would become "Taps" was derived from an old version of the French call "Tattoo" that dated back to at least 1835. Butterfield had his brigade bugler, Oliver Wilcox Norton, play it and adopted it as a call specific to his unit.

It was first played at a military funeral during that same campaign when a cannoneer was killed in action on the forward lines. At the time, military protocol called for firing three volleys at a soldier's burial, but the commanding officer of the artillery unit, Capt. John C. Tidball, was afraid that firing volleys so close to the enemy lines would be mistaken for an attack and would draw return fire from the Confederates. He ordered his bugler to play Butterfield's new call instead.

By 1891, the playing of "Taps" had become a mandatory part of American military funerals, and it has remained so ever since.

A Bell Tolls

*The soldier above all others prays for peace, for it is the soldier who must
suffer and bear the deepest wounds and scars of war.*
–**General Douglas MacArthur**

Under a chill, grey April sky, the remains of a soldier killed in Korea are carried from a brick church in a flag-draped coffin. Late-arriving mourners huddle under umbrellas on the church steps as the procession of official cars wait to make their way to the cemetery. The funeral director's car, in which the minister will ride, will lead the cortege, followed by the hearse and a limousine for the deceased's next-of-kin. A bell tolls mournfully in the church steeple.

Funeral rites are older than civilization itself. Neanderthals interred their dead with loving care, adorning the bodies and burying them with special possessions. Burying soldiers with military honors dates back at least to the ancient Greeks and Romans.

Military funerals are unique in that so many of the rituals and forms are reversed from those of life. Draping a flag over a casket first became a general practice during the Napoleonic Wars more than 200 years ago.

Here, the flag is draped with the blue field of stars to the right, over the left shoulder of the deceased, the only time the flag is properly displayed that way. The casket leaves the church feet-first, and the pallbearers line up in reverse order of military ranking. The only exception to this is when a chaplain dies. The old belief is that a chaplain should always face his flock, and so is carried out headfirst. Committal services for a chaplain are conducted at the foot of the grave.

The flag here has 48 stars, with six horizontal rows of eight each. This was the case from 1912 to 1959, the longest time in our history the flag has remained the same.

In 1959, the flag was changed to 49 stars (seven rows of seven stars) when Alaska entered the U.S. A year later, Hawaii became part of the United States and the familiar 50-star flag (stars in nine rows of stars staggered horizontally and eleven rows of stars staggered vertically) came into being. After a state joins the Union, the number of stars changes on the next fourth of July as per an Executive Order by President James Monroe in 1818.

Swords into Plowshares

They shall beat their swords into plowshares, neither shall they learn war anymore.
—Isaiah 3:4

They left their houses and made their way to the railroad stations, the grade crossings, or the tracks cutting through the fields. Veterans saluted as the train passed by, for it was carrying the remains of a commander-in-chief.

Former General and President Dwight David Eisenhower was the last president to travel to his final resting place by rail. It was early spring in 1969 when the special funeral train carried him from Gettysburg, where he had lived in retirement, to Abilene, Kansas, his birthplace; a warrior returning to the soil.

The accompanying military honor guard is shown here lifting the casket off the train in Abilene for a state funeral, which, in the United States, is given only to a president or one designated by the president to be so honored.

Eisenhower's long rail journey home echoed the final trip of Abraham Lincoln after his assassination in 1865. No American display of public grief ever had or ever would equal Lincoln's extraordinary funeral.

After lying in state in the Capitol, Lincoln's body was taken by train to Philadelphia's Independence Hall before being transported to New York City for an enormous procession and service. On to Albany, across the Great Lakes, the train stopped always in major cities before reaching Chicago. Two weeks after he died, and after millions had paid their last respects, he was finally laid to rest in Springfield, Illinois.

President Franklin D. Roosevelt, who died of a cerebral hemorrhage in 1945 in Warm Springs, Georgia, was also taken to his Washington, D.C. state funeral by train, and, again, millions turned out to watch and pay their respects. A final train journey took him to his burial place in Hyde Park, New York.

In his unprecedented fourth term as Chief Executive, Roosevelt had seen the country through the Great Depression and the Great War.

"I felt as if I knew him," said an unidentified soldier when Roosevelt died. "I felt as if he knew me — and I felt as if he liked me."

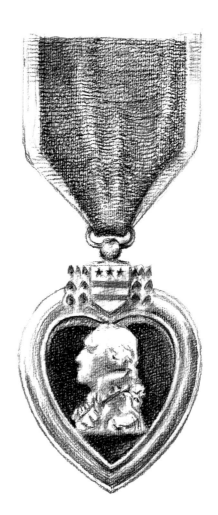

Chapter Eight: Vietnam War

It was as green as this. The air as soft, as sweet. My daughter and I followed along the path of the black marble wall swelling in height and arc with the deaths of soldiers like you. When I found you there, your name, one among so many, I reached up to touch each engraved letter, like a blind person understanding for the first time the life held in a word.

All along the way, the wall was edged with gifts, flowers and feathers and photographs. My daughter left a smooth stone and her second grade school picture. As we walked, we saw ourselves in the wall, our shining day reflected back among the names. I spoke of you. I met you in sixty six, college days. You were brown-eyed, broad-shouldered, handsome, gat-toothed, a scholar, a gentle prankster, everybody's best friend.

I thought of the night I found you in the kitchen, tear-stained and alone, but smiling still for me. "I got my notice," you said. "I think I'm ready to go. I've got to think of it as giving. I just don't know what the gift is."

I guess I know now. The gift to me, to us, to the whole country was you, was all that is young and vibrant and funny and singular and loving and brave.

Today in this peace, I remember you. We all remember.

–Rufus Collinson, "Memorial Day"

VIETNAM WAR 1957–1975

The Vietnam War was America's longest. The war itself began in 1957 and ended in 1975, with U.S. involvement running from 1964 to 1973. Harry Truman introduced The Domino Theory, proposing that if one country fell to Communism, the rest would follow. The next three Presidents – Kennedy, Johnson, and Nixon – espoused this philosophy. Some 2.7 million Americans served in the war, with 58,000 of them killed and 365,000 wounded. South Vietnam lost one million soldiers, and the North Vietnamese lost between 500,000 and one million. Ten million South Vietnamese, half the country's population, became homeless as a result of the war. Three times as many U.S. bombs were dropped as during WW II.

The bombs and chemical defoliants scarred the countryside badly, and in many cases permanently. It was the first war in which the United States failed to achieve its objective. Massive protests at home against what many saw as an immoral war, the war's mounting cost (reflected in mounting taxes), and the high casualty rate shown nightly on television screens created widespread opposition to the war. It was also the first war where returning veterans were at times reviled or ignored.

Purple Heart

Honored

Now the laborer's task is o'er
Now the battle day is past
Father in thy gracious keeping
Leave we now thy servant sleeping.
–John Ellerton, spoken at Franklin D. Roosevelt's funeral.

A detachment of Green Beret Special Forces buries one of its own. A lieutenant leads the procession, with a sergeant following closely behind. Old Glory has two more stars, for Alaska and Hawaii.

Known simply as the Green Berets, the Army's Special Forces unit played a unique role in the Vietnam War. President John F. Kennedy sent 400 Green Berets in 1961 to Vietnam as "Special Adivisors." They trained the Montagnards, the tribal people in the Central Highlands of Vietnam, to fight the Vietcong.

The Montagnards (French for "mountaineers") were subsistence hunter-gatherers and farmers. The men hunted with crossbows and spears, wore loincloths, and lived in small villages of communal longhouses in the mountains. The Vietcong came through their territories, forcing them to perform war-time work and give them food.

The Montagnards wanted to fight back. When they learned of the Special Forces' mission, hundreds of tribesmen begged to be taught how to defend themselves. Ancient surplus guns were handed out, and training began. Within a year, over 200 villages were involved.

By 1964, 18,000 Montagnards were operating out of fortified villages. By 1968, thousands of SF members were leading tens of thousands of tribesmen against the Vietcong. The Special Forces lived with the villagers, patrolled with them, fought with them and sometimes died with them. This created a special bond. The Americans were initiated into the tribes and wore tribal bracelets as a show of brotherhood and commitment. The Green Berets were the only soldiers that the Montagnards ever accepted. It was an emotional time on both sides when the U.S. government pulled them out in the early seventies. One Green Beret said, "They asked me: 'Will you come back?' 'Sure,' we told them, 'we'll be back!' It was the saddest day of my life."

The Army Special Forces continue to be experts in unconventional warfare. They operate behind the lines and depend on close cooperation with the indigenous people. In return, they teach them how to defend themselves. They have to be able to deliver babies, speak several languages, and think in other cultures. They are builders and healers as well as gifted and creative fighters. The Special Forces have been referred to as the "Peace Corps with rifles."

The Special Forces were created in 1952, inspired by the British commandos of World War II. Founder Col. Aaron Bank stated their mission, "to infiltrate by land, sea or air, deep into enemy-occupied territory and organize the resistance/guerilla potential to conduct special forces' operations with emphasis on guerilla warfare."

Soldiers had to be triple volunteers: for the Army, for Airborne, and for Special Forces. Training was unbelievably difficult, and the men that made it were elite warriors. Even so, the rest of the military ignored them. This changed when John F. Kennedy entered the White House. He loved the Special Forces, and his support enabled them to reach their full potential. He also authorized the use of the green beret.

The green beret was inspired by the headgear of the British commandos and soon became a beloved part of the Special Forces gear.

The patch on the beret contains the SF slogan, De Opresso Liber, Latin for "To Free the Oppressed." In addition to the Special Forces shoulder patch, the SF soldier wears a patch shaped like an arrow head to honor the craft and ability of the Native Americans, America's first guerrilla "special forces."

Four Fives

I have no ambition in this world but one and that is to be a fireman. The position may in the eyes of some appear to be a lowly one; but those who know the work which a fireman has to do believe his is a noble calling. Our proudest moment is to save lives. Under the impulse of such thoughts the nobility of the occupation thrills us and stimulates us to deeds of daring even of supreme sacrifice.
—Edward F. Croker, Chief of the New York City Fire Department, 1899-1911

A hero's funeral procession in 1999 for a New York City firefighter and Vietnam veteran killed in the line of duty leaves the church. Fire Department Chaplain, Father Mychal Judge stands at the top of the stairs. Mayor Rudolph Guiliani stands on the stairs on the left side of the painting. Also present are the fire commissioner and the chief of the department, a fire department pipe and drum parade band, and several thousand firefighters.

"Striking the four fives" has been the signal since the 1800s that either a firefighter died in the line of duty or an important person died. Fire department headquarters would transmit five bell strikes, repeated in four series, with a slight pause between each series, followed by the announcement. This was done as long ago as 1865 to inform NYFD firefighters that Abraham Lincoln had died. The custom of "striking the four fives" continues to this day.

When a firefighter dies, mourning bunting is hung at fire headquarters and any firehouse along the funeral route. If the procession passes the deceased's firehouse, a muffled bell is tolled. There are eight pallbearers all of equal height and a color guard made up of four fighters and one captain. The fire chief, company commander, or a friend reads the eulogy.

Fire personnel, color guard and pipe band assemble outside the church before the service's end. The officer in charge commands, "Detail, attention," then "Present arms." The pipe band plays and the pallbearers bring the casket to the hose bed of a Fire Department pumper truck for the final journey to the cemetery.

New York City was settled because of a fire. A Dutch ship went up in flames in 1613, stranding its crew on what was to become Manhattan. Organized firefighting began in 1648 when the First Ordinance established a fire watch of eight wardens and required every male citizen to take a turn. Fires were fought by bucket brigades. The buckets were made of leather by Dutch shoemakers.

The city imported its first two fire engines from England in 1731, but use of buckets didn't end officially until 1819. A central fire bell was placed on City Hall in 1830, and by 1853 the telegraphed system of ringing bells in each firehouse was in place. In 1870, the Fire Department of the City of New York was established; until then it had been comprised mainly of volunteers.

Today the department serves more than eight million people in a 320-square-mile area. There are 12,000 fire officers and firefighters, 3,000 emergency medical technicians, and 1,200 civilian employees. New York's Bravest lost 353 firefighters in the terrorist attack on the World Trade Center on September 11, 2001. Father Mychal Judge was one of the first confirmed dead.

CHAPTER NINE: THE COLD WAR

Now the trumpet summons us again – not as a call to bear arms,
though arms we need – not as a call to battle, though embattled we are
– but a call to bear the burden of a long twilight struggle, year in and
year out, "rejoicing in hope, patient in tribulation"–
a struggle against the common enemies of man: tyranny,
poverty, disease, and war itself.
–John F. Kennedy

THE COLD WAR 1946-1989

In February 4, 1945, in the twilight years of World War II, the leaders of the Allies – U.S. President Franklin D. Roosevelt, British Prime Minister Winston Churchill, and Soviet Premier Josef Stalin – met in the Crimean resort of Yalta.

There the groundwork was laid for the occupation of defeated countries after the war. To Roosevelt and Churchill, that meant reforming those countries into functioning democracies. To Stalin, it meant expansion of the Communist bloc.

By 1946, the war over, the Soviet Union had taken over Eastern Europe, installing Communist governments, and Churchill said, "from Stettin in the Baltic to Trieste in the Adriatic, an Iron Curtain has descended across the continent," to describe the Soviet-enforced separation of East and West. It was an ideological war, pitting Soviet-style socialism against Western democracy and capitalism.

Keeping the two super powers from open warfare were mutual stockpiles of nuclear weapons, and the threat of all-out nuclear war hung over the lives of citizens. The 1962 Cuban Missile Crisis was the closest that both sides came to all-out war, when President John F. Kennedy faced down Soviet Premier Nikita Kruschev over the placement of nuclear arms in Cuba.

Gradually, the two superpowers became less hostile as the Soviet Union slid into economic and political chaos. In 1989, the first Eastern European non-Communist government since World War II took power in Poland. Later that year, the Berlin Wall, symbol of Communist repression, fell. Within two years, the Soviet Union had broken apart into independent republics and the Communist Party was outlawed in Russia.

Without a treaty or a truce, a half-century of conflict had ended.

Handing the Tri-fold Flag

Always Faithful

The muffled drum's sad roll has beat
The soldier's last tattoo;
No more on Life's parade shall meet
That brave and fallen few.
On Fame's eternal camping-ground
Their silent tents are spread,
And Glory guards, with solemn round,
The bivouac of the dead.
–Theodore O'Hara, "The Bivouac of the Dead"

A Border collie guards his master a final time on the hilltop of the family farm. The soldier is a casualty of America's long "shadow" struggle against Communism. Although the term Cold War suggests a conflict without battles, it was not without bloodshed. Several deadly campaigns spanned from the 1940s to the 1980s. Aerial reconnaissance of the Soviet Union alone from 1950 to 1965 caused 107 deaths. Countless dissidents in the Soviet Bloc were killed or imprisoned.

American school children of the fifties and sixties were drilled on what to do in case of an attack. Many people built backyard fall-out shelters. Suspected Communists were banned from some industries, including the entertainment business.

At times the Cold War turned "hot." The Soviet Union fought "proxy" wars, using client states to initiate aggression. The first such confrontation, in Korea, spawned three years of bloody conflict. The Vietnam War claimed another generation of Americans. These East-West conflicts were limited – in territory and weapons. Targets were picked that wouldn't lead to an expansion of the war. They were seen as substitutes to all-out (and most likely nuclear) war.

As the United States and the Soviets vied for world power, they engaged in races in arms and technology. The Soviets were first to put a satellite and then a man in orbit. The Americans were the first to reach the moon. Both nations developed vast intelligence networks, providing the fodder for such movie heroes as James Bond.

Veterans of the Cold War span three generations and include such famous Americans as President Jimmy Carter, Elvis Presley, Ross Perot, former Secretary of State James Baker, Senator Paul Simon, journalist David Broder, actor Chuck Norris, founder of Wendy's Restaurants Dave Thomas, and baseball player Ernie Banks.

Chapter Ten: Persian Gulf War

We'll do okay, because I am with my family; we're brothers.

–An American G.I. before the invasion of Kuwait

PERSION GULF WAR 1991

On August 2, 1990, Iraq invaded its tiny and oil-rich Persian Gulf neighbor, Kuwait. The country fell in a matter of days, and Iraqi president Saddam Hussein ordered his troops to dig in on the northern border of Saudi Arabia.

The United Nations condemned the invasion and authorized a coalition of 39 countries led by the United States to liberate Kuwait.

It was a new kind of war, one waged first and foremost from the air by cruise missiles launched from Navy ships capable of hitting targets from long range with extreme precision, and laser-guided "smart bombs." The air campaign began in January after a long build-up in which nearly a half million American troops were sent to the region.

After destroying Iraq's air defenses, a massive ground assault in February needed only 100 hours to completely rout the Iraqis, who left behind blazing oil fields and massive oil spills.

Estimates of Iraqi dead range up to 100,000, but coalition forces, armed with the latest in high-tech weaponry, suffered only 370 deaths.

For the first time in America's war history, death was not commonplace. With so few lives lost, each loss was felt by the entire nation, with profiles of the victims in the national press and funeral services carried live on cable television news networks. The military funeral, once a local and almost anonymous ceremony, became a national event; a source of sorrow to not just a family, but to a nation.

Marine Loss

Captain of the Corps

The U.S. Military Academy is more than just a university. The experience teaches attention to detail, discipline, loyalty, and unwavering integrity. It is not optional to learn these qualities. You learn them and live them or you leave West Point.

– Capt. Kristin M. Baker, US Army

At a memorial service at the U.S. Military Academy during the Gulf War, the highest-ranking cadet, called the Brigade Commander or Captain of the Corps, places a wreath at the base of the Sylvanus Thayer Memorial statue. A line of classmates salute at attention.

For the first time in the history of West Point, a woman represents the Corps of Cadets. She is Kristin Baker, who was chosen by the commanding officers of America's oldest military academy to lead the Corps during the 1989-90 academic year.

It is a great and singular honor, recognizing not just intelligence or physical prowess, but leadership ability. Others who have been Captain of the Corps include Robert E. Lee, John J. Pershing, and Douglas MacArthur.

Although wars have been fought by men primarily, women have distinguished themselves on the battlefield and as leaders of armies since early times. The Greeks as early as the fifth century B.C. wrote about female conquerors, admirals, and defenders of cities.

Boadicea, Queen of the Britons, led a revolt against Roman occupation in the early third century A.D. and remains a great British heroine. Perhaps the most famous of all female warriors was Joan of Arc, the French peasant girl who saved 15th century France from the English.

In America, there are many records of women dressing as men to serve in every war from the Revolution on, and, in the 18th and 19th centuries, women often followed their men as they marched to war.

By World War II, tens of thousands of women served their country in the various women's service branches. It was not until relatively recent times, however, that women were finally admitted into the regular armed forces as full equals to men.

In 1976, three years after the draft was abolished and the nation turned to an all-volunteer army, women were admitted to America's service academies. In 1973, only 1.6 percent of all military personnel were women. By 1990, that number had risen to more than ten percent – 15 percent of whom are officers.

Today women are company commanders and pilots, astronauts and administrators, privates and generals, and, although they are still excluded from combat roles, the barriers against women are crumbling along with the attitudes that created them. Leading the crusade against these barriers and attitudes are the service academies, where leaders like Kristin Baker are allowed and encouraged to be all that they can be.

There to Abide

The Lord is my shepherd: I shall not want
He maketh me to lie down in green pastures: he leadeth me beside the still waters.
He restoreth my soul: he leadeth me in the paths of righteousness for his name's sake.
Yea, though I walk through the valley of the shadow of death, I will fear no evil: for thou art with me:
thy rod and thy staff they comfort me.

−Psalm Twenty-Three

A preacher conducts a funeral service in this rural Mississippi church that was built by its parishioners. A grandfather kneels at the casket of a United States Marine helicopter gunner who died in Kuwait. The pallbearers, men and women from the gunner's company, stand to the left rear. After the service, old spirituals such as "Just a Closer Walk With Thee," "How I Got Over," "The Storm is Passing Over," "Swing Low, Sweet Chariot," "Nearer My God to Thee," and "Down By the Riverside" will be sung.

The Persian Gulf War garnered support in a way that had not been seen in Amercia since World War II. Most public opinion polls showed that 90 percent of Americans approved of the United States' involvement. Tens of thousands of Americans wrote letters of support to unknown soldiers, and sent packages of food, clothing, music and sunblock lotion.

The history of the U.S. Marine Corps dates back to November 10, 1775 when the Continental Congress established "two Battalions of Marines…to be good seamen, or so acquainted with maritime affairs as to be able to serve to advantage by sea, when required." The Marines were originally under Navy regulations while on the water and under the Army Articles of War while on land. Congress ended this confusion in 1834 by assigning the Marine Corps to the Navy, but as its own separate service.

In the Revolutionary War, the Marines fought against the British on John Paul Jones' ships. They made their first amphibious landing on the shores of the Bahamas in 1776.

Marines participated in dozens of "scattered actions" in all parts of the world throughout the 1800s. They made a 600-mile desert march from Egypt to topple the Barbary Pirate stronghold in Tripoli, ending the war in the Mediterranean. This led the unknown author of "The Marines Hymn" to write, "from the halls of Montezuma, to the shores of Tripoli/we fight our country's battles in the air, on land and on the sea." Another line from that song, "We have fought in every clime and place/ where we could take a gun," was well lived. Marines fought in Brooklyn, Haiti, Cuba, the Galapagos, Puerto Rico, Greece, the Philippines, Antarctica, China, Mexico, Panama, and the Fiji Islands, prompting Richard Harding Davis' famous quote, "the Marines have landed and have the situation well in hand."

The Marine nickname "leatherneck" originated from a black leather collar worn around the neck that protected the jugular from the slash of a bayonet, spear, or sword.

Marine lieutenant colonel Pete Ellis, a brilliant tactician, formulated the basis for the entire American WW II campaign in the Pacific, and Allied landings in North Africa and Europe. He called for amphibious forces that would create new bases for the Navy, utilizing surprise and lightning execution. Marines have been an integral part of every major conflict of the 20th century. The Marines were in first during the Gulf War and General Norman Schwarzkopf said, "if I use words like brilliant, it would really be an underdescription."

Morning Reconnaissance

That's the difference — we are no different. We do the job the same. No better, no worse than they do.

—1st Lt. Carrie Howell, U.S.A.F. fighter pilot

At dawn in the Middle East, a female fighter pilot strides to a plane which is armed and ready. The fighter jet has no preference for who sits at the controls, but for most of the twentieth century, society did.

In the beginning, in World War I, American military pilots were male and white. In World War II, African-Americans, most notably the famed Tuskegee airmen, won the right to hold one of the most prestigious, and dangerous, jobs in the military.

It was not until 1973 that the Navy became the first service branch to welcome women into its flight school. Within the next several years, the Army and, finally, the Air Force, followed.

Another twenty years passed before President Bill Clinton signed an executive order that cleared women to fly close combat missions, a role they have carried out with distinction in Iraq, Kosovo, and Afghanistan. Lt. Col. Martha McSally was the first female pilot to fly an official combat sortie.

There were, however, women pilots who performed with great bravery and skill during World War II. They served in the Soviet Union, pressed into service out of necessity when the Germans invaded their country.

Flying out-dated, single-engine biplanes, the Russian women fought off Luftwaffe bombers. Two of the pilots, Lilya Litvak and Katya Budanova, earned status as aces before they were killed in action.

Even in World War I, two Russian women, Princess Eugenie Shakhovskaya and Princess Sophie Alesandrovna Dolgorunaya, were military pilots.

The first American woman to hold a pilot's license of any kind was Harriet Quimby in 1911. Even though women volunteered for World War I, the American military accepted none. During World War II, American women were allowed to pilot nearly every type of aircraft. These aviators, known as WASPs, flew transports, towed target aircraft used in gunnery training, and even served as test pilots, but they were not considered official military pilots.

At the beginning of the 21st century, the Air Force had more than 300 female pilots and another 100 navigators. In 1999, Air Force Col. Eileen Collins became the first woman to command a space shuttle mission.

With more women flying, the controversy that once surrounded them has all but disappeared. Asked once about differences between male and female pilots, Rear Adm. Alfred Harms replied: "On any given day I don't have a clue who is in which aircraft, and frankly it doesn't matter. They are absolutely one and the same."

RFletcher

CHAPTER ELEVEN: AFGHANISTAN WAR

There are those who teach only the sweet lessons of peace and safety;
But I teach lessons of war and death to those I love,
That they readily meet invasions, when they come.

—Walt Whitman

AFGHANISTAN WAR 2001-

On September 11, 2001, Islamic extremists captured four U.S. airplanes. Two were flown into the twin towers of the World Trade Center in New York, leading to their collapse and the loss of more than 3,000 lives. Another struck the Pentagon, killing more than 200. The fourth crashed in Pennsylvania, its hijackers overpowered by heroic passengers.

The hijackers were disciples of Osama bin Laden, the leader of a terrorist network known as Al Qaeda. Bin Laden has been sheltered by the fundamentalist Taliban regime that held Afghanistan in an iron grip of militant fanaticism.

America's first war of the 21st century was a very different kind of conflict. The enemy was not another country, but a shadowy network of terrorists whose leaders could melt into the forbidding mountains of Afghanistan. But they were also scattered across the globe, communicating by satellite phones and the internet, sometimes blending in with their neighbors, living seemingly ordinary lives while planning extraordinary acts of terrorism.

America's elite forces led an international effort operating with the endorsement of the United Nations. They included: Navy Seals; Green Berets, Rangers, and the elite Delta Force of the Army; Special Ops from the Air Force; and, as always, the Marines.

It was not officially called a war, but that's what it was – a war without set battles or a clearly defined end.

Delta Force

Friendly Fire

Let every nation know, whether it wishes us well or ill, that we shall pay any price,
bear any burden, meet any hardship, support any friend, oppose any foe to assure
the survival and the success of liberty.
–John F Kennedy

Until September 11, 2001, terrorism, for Americans, had always been something that happened somewhere else.

But on that day, branded as vividly into the minds of a generation of Americans as the Japanese sneak attack on Pearl Harbor sixty years earlier, were the indelible scenes on our shores witnessed by all America.

President George W. Bush assured our nation that America would fight back and a united America will win. An immediate national priority was established to prevent further attack and to protect our home front.

A platoon of special forces stands at attention having recovered the bodies of three of their own and a Northern Alliance freedom fighter. The bodies were hand carried on stretchers from the front line to a relatively safe zone away from direct enemy fire. This short ceremony will conclude when the bodies are air-lifted by helicopter to an airfield where a transport will bring the flag-covered caskets home to America.

In the relatively short time since the Gulf War, Americans have come to expect bombs to strike with pinpoint accuracy. It is shocking to hear that a bomb or missile has missed its target.

Sometimes, the misses come with tragic consequences, either to local civilians or American troops. Such was the case on December 4, 2001, when what the military calls an "errant piece of ordnance" dropped by a B-52 killed three Green Berets during the battle to take Kandahar, one of the last concentrations of Taliban military strength.

The dead were Master Sgt. Jefferson D. Davis, Sgt. 1st Class Daniel H. Petithory, and Staff Sgt. Brian C. Prosser, all with the 5th Special Forces Group. They died doing their duty, fighting, as President Bush would say, "for a noble and just cause."

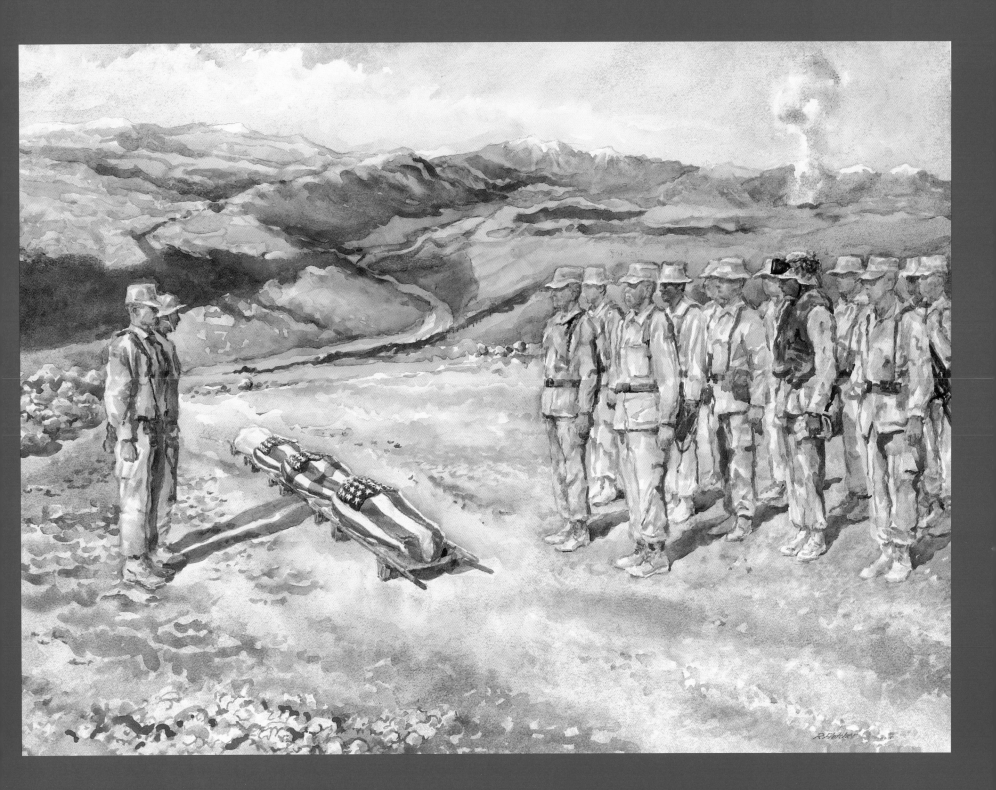

CHAPTER ELEVEN: PRESENT DAY

*They have come forward from city and farm whenever they have been needed
for over 200 years. No group of Americans has a greater claim to the love,
appreciation and respect of fellow citizens than the warriors of the nation.
They are sons and daughters and brothers and sisters, husbands and wives.
And they fight the nation's wars for us, not as strangers but as our very own.
They are the pride of America – the best the nation has to offer.*

—General Colin Powell

More than 26 million veterans of the U.S. Armed Forces are alive today, and about one-quarter of all Americans (70 million people) are eligible for Government veterans' benefits. Almost half of all Americans who served during wartime in our country's history are still living, and nearly 80 percent of today's veterans served during a war.

There are 16 million veterans of World War II. Half a million of them die each year, an average of 1,100 a day.

There are currently 26,000 American Legion and Veterans of Foreign War posts in the U.S.

Since January 1, 2000, any family requesting military services for a veteran's funeral has received it. Only nine percent of veterans' families request funeral honors. The Department of Defense, however, estimates that this figure will reach 45 percent as each day 1,500 more veterans die.

As a nation, we have learned how vital it is to remember, to celebrate the veterans who are still alive and to mourn the loss of so many soldiers who have departed. Every year millions of people take part in Memorial Day or Veterans Day parades, visit "the Wall" (the Vietnam Memorial), the Arlington National Cemetery (where veterans of every war are buried and fifteen funerals are held daily), the National D-Day Memorial in Virginia, or simply a local cemetery.

The POW/MIA movement is still strong. The search continues for some 88,000 military personnel whose whereabouts remain unknown.

At The Parade

Memorial Day

Walk softly about this place. They have gone into the tent for the night, their heads on pillows of dust, their arms stacked, their march ended, their battle fought. Sleep on, great boat, till the morning light strikes through the rifts of the tents and the trumpet sounds the reveille of the Resurrection.

—Rev. De Witt Talmadge, Decoration Day service at Arlington, 1873

A family holds a picnic next to a rural community cemetery after the morning's Memorial Day services. Every year on the last Monday in May, America remembers the 1.4 million men and women who died in 60 military actions spanning more than two centuries. Parades of soldiers and bands mark the day on land, and services are held on ships for those who died at sea. Some 625,000 Americans were killed in the twentieth century alone, although less than one percent of those died after 1975.

More than twenty cities and towns in the U.S. claim to be the birthplace of Memorial Day. Sometime near the end of the Civil War, there was a strong, national need to remember and honor the dead. On April 26, 1866, women of Columbus, Mississippi, decorated the graves of both Confederate and Union soldiers who had fallen at the Battle of Shiloh. Two years before in Boalsburg, Pennsylvania, Emma Hunter placed flowers on the tomb of her father, a colonel in the Union Army. She met another woman at the cemetery whose son had died in the war. They agreed to meet the following year to decorate the graves of their loved ones.

The village of Waterloo, New York, held a Memorial Day celebration on May 5, 1866. In 1966, Congress and President Lyndon B. Johnson declared Waterloo the "birthplace" of Memorial Day.

The Grand Army of the Republic, a Union veterans' association, organized a ceremony at Arlington Cemetery on May 30, 1868 and called it Decoration Day. General John Alexander Logan issued General Order No. 11, which created Decoration Day. It read in part, "Let no neglect, no ravages of time, testify to the present or coming generations that we have forgotten as a people the cost of a free and undivided republic."

The name was changed to Memorial Day in 1888. It was a legal holiday in the North, but the South honored their dead on different days.

It wasn't until after World War I that the day was expanded to honor soldiers killed in all wars. Memorial Day was declared a national holiday in 1971, even though it is sometimes still called Decoration Day.

Oliver Wendell Holmes Jr. felt that Memorial Day celebrated and solemnly reaffirmed "a national act of enthusiasm and faith."

"To fight out a war," he said, "you must believe something and want something with all your might. So must you do to carry anything else to an end worth reaching. More than that, you must be willing to commit yourself to a course, perhaps a long and hard one, without being able to foresee exactly where you will come out. The rest belongs to fate."

Grand Marshal

From these honored dead we take increased devotion to that cause for
which they gave the last full measure of devotion; that we here highly resolve
that these dead shall not have died in vain; that this nation, under God,
shall have a new birth of freedom; and that government of the people, by the
people, for the people, shall not perish from the Earth.
—Abraham Lincoln, Gettysburg Address

The Grand Marshal prepares to lead the annual parade on Memorial Day at 11 A.M. in Warwick, New York. Nicholas P. Lesando rose to the rank of Senior Master Sergeant in the Air Force and served his country during WW II, Korea and Vietnam. The Nicholas P. Lesando Jr. Warwick American Legion Post 214 is named after his son Nicholas, who was killed in action in Vietnam. Nick Sr. has served as post commander for 14 years and officer of the post for 40 years.

Every year in towns and villages throughout the country, Memorial Day is observed. American Legion and VFW members, Girl Scouts, Boy Scouts, the local high school marching band and townspeople gather for a parade and a wreath-laying ceremony at the local cemetery. At noon a memorial flag at a local park is raised from half-mast to full staff, and all return to the Legion Hall for cold drinks and hot dogs.

The American Legion is the largest veterans' organization in the United States. It began as an idea generated by four soldiers in Paris in late January, 1919, at the end of World War I. General Pershing gave his blessing, and March 13-15, 1919, is recognized as the birth dates of the American Legion. Later that year, the Legion was chartered by Congress as a "patriotic, mutual-help, war-time veterans organization."

The organization advocates for veterans, continues military friendships, and helps disabled veterans get the care they need. The Legion is actively involved in communities, sponsoring Boy Scout troops, junior baseball leagues, and supplying medical equipment where it is needed. During the Depression, the American Legion helped over one million men find jobs. The Legion also helped write the GI Bill of Rights after WWII.

There are currently 2.7 million members in nearly 15,000 American Legion Posts worldwide. Any person who was in the U.S. Armed Forces during World War I, World War II, Korean War, Vietnam War, Lebanon/Grenada, Panama, and the Persian Gulf War is eligible for membership. Their motto is "For God and Country."

At one of the first Memorial Day ceremonies, Oliver Wendell Holmes said: "On this day when we decorate their graves – the dead come back and live with us. I see them now, more than I can number, as once I saw them on this Earth. They are the same bright figures that come also before your eyes; and when I speak of those who were my brothers, the same words describe yours. We have seen the best and noblest of our generation pass away."

The Sentinel

It was as though something had pulled at me. A voice seemed to say: "This is a pal of yours"
—Sgt. Edward F. Younger, explaining how he chose the Unknown Soldier from World War I

"Here rests in honored glory an American soldier known but to God." These famous words are inscribed on the Tomb of the Unknowns, also known as the Tomb of the Unknown Soldier, at Arlington National Cemetery in Virginia.

Standing atop a hill overlooking Washington, D.C., the east panel of the white marble sarcophagus has three sculpted Greek figures representing Peace, Victory, and Valor. Below is the grave of the World War I Unknown. The crypts of unknowns from World War II, Korea, and Vietnam are marked with white marble slabs flush with the plaza to the west.

Four World War I unknowns were exhumed in France on Memorial Day, 1921. On October 24, Sergeant Younger, wounded in combat and recipient of the Distinguished Service Medal, chose the third casket from the left: "I put the rose on the coffin in front of me and went back into the sunlight. I still remember the awed feeling I had, standing there alone."

The Unknown Soldier lay in state in the Capitol Rotunda on a catafalque that had borne the bodies of three assassinated presidents – Lincoln, Garfield, and McKinley – and would later bear a fourth, John F. Kennedy.

On Armistice Day, November 11, 1921, President Warren G. Harding, accompanied by General Pershing, officiated at the internment ceremonies. The president declared: "As we return this poor clay to its mother soil, garlanded by love and covered with the decorations that only nations can bestow, I can sense the prayers of our people, of all peoples, that this Armistice Day shall mark the beginning of a new and lasting era, of peace on earth, good-will among men."

The Unknowns from World War II and Korea were interred at the same time on Memorial Day, May 30, 1958. Caissons carried them to Arlington, where President Eisenhower awarded each the Medal of Honor as 212 of the 320 living Medal of Honor recipients looked on.

The Vietnam Unknown was interred on Memorial Day in 1984 by President Ronald Reagan. After presenting the Medal of Honor, Reagan said: "Today, we pause, to embrace him and all who served us so well in a war whose end offered no parades, no flags, and so little thanks…Let us, if we must, debate the lessons learned at some other time. Today we simply say with pride: Thank you, dear son, and may God cradle you in His loving arms."

The remains of the Vietnam Unknown were exhumed May 14, 1998 and returned to his family after DNA testing was able to determine his identity.

Sentinels of the "Old Guard," which traces its roots back to the Revolutionary War, watch over the Unknowns 24 hours a day, 365 days a year, in all weather conditions. Becoming a Tomb Guard is an incredibly rigorous process: There have been only 500 tomb guards since the 3rd Infantry "President's Own" began their duty in 1948.

The Tomb Guard paces a 63-foot-long black mat between the Tomb and the plaza steps. The Guard marches 21 steps from one end to the other, turns to face the tomb and stands at attention for exactly 21 seconds. The Sentinel's Creed proclaims, "this soldier will in Honored Glory rest under my eternal vigilance."

4th of July Band Concert

Duty, honor, country: Those three hallowed words reverently dictate what you ought to be, what you can be, what you will be. They are your rallying point to build courage when courage seems to fail, to regain faith when there seems to be little cause for faith, to create hope when hope becomes forlorn.

–General Douglas MacArthur

Veterans, families, and cadets enjoy the annual Fourth of July band concert at sunset at West Point Military Academy in New York. West Point occupies 16,000 acres on the west bank of the Hudson River, which begins 300 miles to the North at Lake Tear-of-the-Clouds and ends 50 miles south in New York Harbor. The Hudson River is a tidal estuary and the currents can be seen reflecting on the surface in the twilight glow. The two high points visible on the river are Storm King Mountain and Breakneck Ridge, part of the beautiful Hudson Highlands.

The concert starts at 8 P.M. but many families arrive in the afternoon and picnic on the lawn under the large elms, planted over 180 years ago while Sylvanus Thayer, the "Father of the Military Academy," was superintendent.

More than 4,000 cadets and 12,000 visitors are gathered in front of the Trophy Point Band Shell. West Point cadets are seated in three groups closest to the band shell. Cadets arrive in military formation. All four classes (each roughly 1,200 members) are there – the freshmen "Plebes," sophomore "Yearlings," junior "Cows," and senior 'Firsties." The Plebes are getting a rare break from their rigorous six-week "Beast Barracks" training.

The people to the right in the painting are seated on the steps of Battle Monument, a memorial to those killed during the Civil War. A forty-six foot shaft of solid granite, it is the largest polished stone monument in the world. West Point played a major role in the Civil War, supplying 290 Union generals and 150 Confederate generals.

The British sailed upriver in 1777 and burned Kingston, where the "government-on-the-run" was located after vacating New York City. In response, a great iron chain was forged in 1778 at the Sterling Iron Works in Orange County and stretched across the Hudson from West Point to Constitution Island (pictured to the right in the painting). The Great Chain was 600 yards long, had links two feet in length, and weighed 65 tons.

West Point is the oldest military college in the United States. It transitioned from a fort to an academy in 1802, when Thomas Jefferson appointed the first ten cadets. The Long Gray Line (gray was used initially because it was less expensive than blue) is for today's cadets a "linkage from cadets of two hundred years ago with the cadets of two hundred years from now," says General David Palmer.

Congressman Jack Reed, a West Point graduate, said: "Life at West Point begins before dawn and lasts forever." Famous graduates include two men who walked on the moon, two Presidents – Grant and Eisenhower – and Generals MacArthur, Lee, Patton, Sheridan, Bradley, and Schwartzkopf.

More than 100 graduates of West Point have been U.S. Olympians and three have won the Heisman trophy. "West Point gave me more than a military career," General Norman Schwarzkopf said, "it gave me a calling."

Former superintendent General MacArthur returned in 1962 two years before he died and said, "In the evening of my memory, always I come back to West Point. Always there echoes and re-echoes Duty – Honor – Country. When I cross the river my last conscious thoughts will be of The Corps, and The Corps, and The Corps."

Three Generations

We have shared the incommunicable experience of war; we have felt, we still feel, the passion of life to its top.

–Oliver Wendell Holmes, Jr

The Stewart family, three generations of soldiers, prepare to march in the Memorial Day parade in Warwick, New York. Sergeant First Class (Retired) Robert Stewart Sr. poses with six sons and one grandson. The family has reunited to serve as honor guard in the parade for more than twenty years. In 2002, Robert Stewart Sr. was the Grand Marshal. The family members are left to right: Robert Sr., Robert Jr., Paul Sr., Timothy, James Sr., Ralph, Alexander, and Paul Jr.

Sergeant First Class (Retired) Robert P. Stewart Sr. is a Korean War veteran. He attended Airborne School and served in the 11th Airborne Division at Fort Campbell, Kentucky. He retired from the reserves in 1992 and has been a member of the American Legion for more than 50 years. He has eleven children – seven boys and four girls.

Staff Sergeant (Retired) Robert P. Stewart Jr. is a graduate of the U.S. Army Jump Master School. He is a veteran of Operation Fury in Grenada, Operation Desert Shield and Desert Storm.

Gunnery Sergeant (Retired) Paul H. Stewart Sr. joined the Marines in 1975. He is a veteran of the Persian Gulf War.

Sergeant (Retired) Timothy R. Stewart joined the Army in 1978. After serving in Puerto Rico, West Point, Holland and Germany, he returned to the United States and performed veterinary services at Fort Belvoir, Virginia.

Lieutenant Colonel James E. Stewart Sr. is the highest-ranking member of the family. A 1985 graduate of the United States Military Academy at West Point, he is a Persian Gulf War veteran. A graduate of Command and General Staff College, he is currently the Operations Officer for the 4th Brigade, 75th Division. He has earned the Parachutist Badge and the prestigious Bronze Star.

Sergeant First Class (Retired) Ralph H. Stewart served in Korea, Germany, Fort Ord, California and Fort Dix, New Jersey. His last assignment was to the 1st Region, 2nd Brigade, ROTC Command.

Sergeant Alexander A. Stewart joined the Army in 1984. His posts included Korea and Germany.

Sergeant Paul H. Stewart Jr. is currently assigned to Marine Corps Base, 29 Palms, California.

Military families have a long tradition. Mrs. Bixby of Boston lost five sons in the Civil War. Albert and Louise Wood of Port Washington, New York, saw four of their five sons enlist in World War II and all of them return safely.

Five Sullivan brothers from Waterloo, Iowa enlisted in the Navy during World War II. On November 13, 1942, the cruiser they were on was hit and sunk. All of the brothers died. The Navy awarded them Purple Hearts posthumously and christened a new destroyer The Sullivans. Their only sister, Genevieve, enlisted in the Navy as a WAVE. Franklin D. Roosevelt told Mrs. Sullivan: "As one of your sons wrote, 'We will make a team together that can't be beat.' It is this spirit which in the end must triumph." The movie *Saving Private Ryan* is loosely based on the Sullivans' story.

The Stewarts' parade tradition continues to this day. The only change? In the beginning, Robert Sr. counted off the cadence. Now it is Lieutenant Colonel James Stewart who steps off the color guard and the parade.

"I taught my family to always do the right thing and to serve their country with honor," said Robert Stewart Sr., "That's the way I was brought up by my father, Alex Stewart. By the way, we'll all be at the parade next year."

Placing the Flag

On this Veterans Day . . . let us pray that there will be no veterans of any further wars, not because all shall have perished but because all shall have learned to live together in peace. And to the dead here, in this cemetery, we say they are the race, they are the race immortal.
—John F. Kennedy, Nov. 11 1961

Clayton Eurich, a World War II veteran and VFW member, places flags on the graves of veterans from the Revolutionary War to WW II three weeks before Veterans Day. The early morning frost in the shadows has not yet melted. The Sugar Maples are in full fall color. Soon frost will seal the flags in the ground until Memorial Day, when they will be replaced by new ones.

Clayton Eurich served in the Navy amphibious force from 1943 to 1946. He is a former commander of Warwick, New York's VFW Post 4662, and is currently the chaplain. Mr. Eurich has been active as a Boy Scout Scoutmaster and Council Coordinator for almost forty years.

The Old Guard does a similar service to all veterans' graves in Arlington Cemetery. An American flag is placed precisely the measure of a boot away from each headstone. This tradition is called "flags in." National ceremonies for Veterans Day take place every year at the Tomb of the Unknowns and are often presided over by the President.

The Veterans of Foreign Wars of the United States has its roots in 1899 and is the oldest major veterans organization in America. There are 1.8 million members at 12,000 posts. The VFW preserves veterans' rights, advocates a strong national defense, promotes patriotism and offers community service. The VFW has helped pass GI Bills for three generations of war vets, helped make the Star Spangled Banner the national anthem, and provides $2.6 million in college scholarships every year.

The VFW was the first organization to launch a national, annual distribution of the Buddy Poppy, hand-made by disabled veterans. Since 1922, the Buddy Poppy has been sold by veterans to raise funds for needy and disabled veterans, dependents of veterans, and orphans of deceased veterans. The poppy movement was inspired by Canadian medical officer John McCrae's famous WW I poem "In Flanders Field" (see World War I chapter). McCrae wrote of his experiences, "It was hell all the time. We really expected to die in our tracks. We never had our boots off, much less our clothes."

In 1926, Congress officially dubbed November 11 Armistice Day and it became a legal national holiday in 1938. This was to recognize the end of "the War to end all wars" on the 11th hour of the 11th day of the 11th month in 1918. It was at this time that November 11-18 became known as Veterans Week. After World War II and Korea, Congress in 1956 changed the name from Armistice Day to Veterans Day to honor all veterans. President Eisenhower wrote, "let us solemnly remember the sacrifices of all those who fought so valiantly to preserve our heritage of freedom and let us reconsecrate ourselves to the task of promoting an enduring peace so that their efforts shall not be in vain." Great Britain and France celebrate November 11 as Armistice Day, while Canada observes it as Remembrance Day.

Veterans Day everywhere is a day of parades and speeches. At 11 A.M. a flag is lowered and raised as church bells ring after two minutes of silence, just as they did in 1918.

O My Son, My Son

Executive Mansion,
November 21, 1864

Dear Madam:

I have been shown in the files of the War Department a statement of the Adjutant-General of Massachusetts that you are the mother of five sons who have died gloriously on the field of battle.

I feel how weak and fruitless must be any words of mine which should attempt to beguile you from the grief of a loss so overwhelming. But I cannot refrain from tendering to you the consolation that may be found in the thanks of the Republic they died to save.

I pray that our heavenly Father may assuage the anguish of your bereavement, and leave you only the cherished memory of the loved and lost, and the solemn pride that must be yours to have laid so costly a sacrifice upon the altar of freedom.

Yours very sincerely and respectfully,

A. Lincoln

Abraham Lincoln

Dedicated to all veterans of all wars and all who love them

Bibliography

Alcott, L. M. *Hospital Sketches.* Boston: James Redpath Publishers, 1863.

Allen, Oliver E. New York, New York: *A History of the World's Most Exhilarating and Challenging City. New York:* Atheneum, 1990.

Andrews, Owen. *Arlington National Cemetery: A Moment of Silence.* Photography by Cameron Davidson. Washington: The Preservation Press, 1994.

Andrews, Peter. *In Honored Glory: The Story of Arlington.* G.P. Putnam's Sons, 1966.

Angle, Paul M. *A Pictorial History of the Civil War Years.* New York: Doubleday and Company, 1967.

Associated Press, writers and photographers. *World War II: A 50th Anniversary History.* New York: Henry Holt and Co., 1989.

Axelrod, Alan. *The Complete Idiot's Guide to the American Revolution.* Indianapolis: Alpha Books, 2000.

Baily, Ronald H. and the Editors of Time-Life Books. *World War II.* Alexandria: Time-Life Books, 1977.

Bigler, Philip. *In Honored Glory -- Arlington National Cemetery: The Final Post.* Arlington: Vandamere Press, 1986.

Bliven, Bruce Jr. *New York: A Bicentennial History.* New York: W.W. Norton and Company, 1981.

Burrows, Edwin G. and Mike Wallace. *Gotham: A History of New York City to 1898.* New York: Oxford University Press, 1999.

Carter III, Samuel. *The Last Cavaliers: Confederate and Union Cavalry in the Civil War.* New York: St. Martin's Press, 1979.

Coffin, Margaret M. *Death in Early America.* Nashville: Thomas Nelson Publishers, 1976.

Commager, Henry Steele and Richard B. Morris, eds. *The Spirit of 'Seventy-Six: The Story of the American Revolution as Told by Participants.* New York: Harper and Row, 1958.

Daniels, Roger. *Coming to America: A History of Immigration and Ethnicity in American Life.* New York: HarperCollins, 1990.

Drury, Ian. *Confederate Infantryman: 1861-1865.* Osprey Military, 1993.

Ellis, John. *Cavalry: The History of Mounted Warfare.* G.P.Putnam's Sons, 1978.

Fennelly, Catherine. *Life in an Old New England Country Village.* New York: Thomas Y. Crowell, 1969.

Fisher, Margaret, Mary Jane Fowler and Jerry J. Jennings. *Colonial America.* Grand Rapids: The Fideler Company, 1974.

Fredericks, Pierce G. *The Yanks Are Coming.* New York: Bantam Books, 1964.

Gawne, Jonathan. *Over There! The American Soldier in World War I.* London: Greenhill Books, 1997. [also Stackpole Books, Harrisburg]

Grant, John, James M. Lynch and Ronald H. Bailey. *West Point: The First 200 Years.* Guilford (CT): Globe Pequot Press, 2002.

Gray, Thomas. *Elegy Written in a Country Church Yard and Other Poems.* Robert Carter and Brothers, 1853.

Gurney, Gene. *Arlington National Cemetery: A Picture Story of America's Most Famous Burial Grounds from the Civil War to President John F. Kennedy's Burial.* New York: Crown Publishing, 1965.

Habenstein, Robert W. and William M. Lamers. *The History of American Funeral Directing.* Brookfield, WI: National Funeral Directors Association, 2001.

Haines, Francis. *Horses in America.* New York: Thomas Y. Crowell, 1971.

Hass, Kristin Ann. *Carried to the Wall: American Memory and the Vietnam Veterans Memorial.* Berkeley: University of California Press, 1998.

Hawke, David Freeman. *Everyday Life in Early America. New York: Harper and Row, 1988.*

Hinkel, John Vincent. *Arlington: Monument to Heroes.* New York: Prentice-Hall, Inc., 1970.

Hoare, Robert. R.J. Unstead, ed. *World War Two: An Illustrated History in Colour 1939-1945.* London: MacDonald Educational, 1973.

Holmes, Oliver Wendell, Jr. *Touched With Fire: Civil War Letters and Diary.* Cambridge: Harvard University Press, 1946.

Horne, A.D., ed. *The Wounded Generation: America After Vietnam.* New York: Prentice-Hall, 1981.

Jackson, Charles O, ed. Passing: *The Vision of Death in America.* Westport: Greenwood Press, 1977.

Johnson, J.R. and A.H. Bill. *Horsemen Blue and Gray – A Pictorial History.* New York: Oxford University Press, 1960.

Jones, Constance. R.I.P. *The Complete Book of Death and Dying.* New York: Harper Collins, 1997.

Kalman, Bobbie. *The Early Family Home.* Toronto: Crabtree Publishing, 1982.

Katcher, Philip. *American Civil War Armies: State Troops.* London: Osprey Publishing, 1986.

Katcher, Philip. *American Civil War Armies: Union Artillery, Cavalry and Infantry.* Osprey Publishing, 1986.

Katcher, Philip. *The U.S. Army 1890-1920.* London: Osprey Publishing, 1986.

Ketchum, Richard M. ed., and the Editors of American Heritage. *The American Heritage Picture History of the Civil War.* New York: American Heritage Publishing Co., 1960.

Mack, William P. and Royal W. Connell. *Naval Ceremonies, Customs, and Traditions, 5th Edition.* Bethesda: Naval Institute Press, 1980.

Maisel, Albert. *They All Chose America.* New York: Thomas Nelson and Sons, 1957.

Marlowe, George Francis. *Churches of Old New England.* New York: The Macmillan Co., 1947.

Marshall, S.L.A. and the Editors of American Heritage. *The American Heritage History of World War I.* New York: American Heritage Publishing, 1964.

McAfee, Michael J. and John P. Langellier. Billy Yank: *The Uniform of the Union Army, 1861-1865.* London: Greenhill Books, 1996.

Merrill, James M. *Spurs to Glory: The Story of the United States Cavalry.* Chicago: Rand McNally and Co., 1966.

Mossman, B.C. and M.W. Stark. *Last Salute: Civil and Military Funerals, 1921-1969,* Washington: Dept. of the Army, 1971.

Murphy, Richard W. *The Nation Reunited: War's Aftermath.* Alexandria: Time-Life Books, 1987.

Nardo, Don. *The War of 1812.* San Diego: Lucent Books, 1991.

Neumann, George C. *Swords and Blades of the American Revolution.* Harrisburg: Stackpole Books, 1976.

Neumann, George C. and Frank J. Kravic. *Collector's Illustrated Encyclopedia of the American Revolution.* Harrisburg: Stackpole Books, 1975.

O'Connor, Thomas H. *Civil War Boston: Home Front and Battlefield.* Boston: Northeastern University Press, 1997.

Peterson, Harold L. *The Book of the Continental Soldier.* Harrisburg: Stackpole Books, 1968.

Quarrie, Bruce. *Special Forces: The Elite Military Units of the World.* Chartwell Books, 1990.

Rankin, Robert H. *Uniforms of the Army.* New York: G.P. Putnam's Sons, 1967.

Richards, Maurice and Michael Moody. *The First World War: Ephemera, Momentos, Documents.* London: Jupiter Books, 1975.

Rodenbough, Theo F., ed., *The Photographic History of the Civil War: The Cavalry.* New York: The Fairfax Press, 1983.

Rose, Harold Wickliffe. *The Colonial Houses of Worship in America.* New York: Hastings House, 1963.

Roth, David M. *Connecticut: A Bicentennial History.* New York: W.W. Norton, 1979.

Schauffler, Robert, ed. *Our Flag in Verse and Prose,* Dodd, Mead and Company, 1924

Schortemeier, Frederick E. Rededicating *America: Life and Recent Speeches of Warren G. Harding.* Indianapolis: Bobbs-Merrill, 1920.

Sochurek, Howard. "Viet Nam's Montagnards: Caught in the Jaws of a War," *National Geographic.* April, 1968.

Smith, Chard Powers. *The Housatonic: Puritan River.* New York: Rinehart and Company, 1946.

Smith, Whitney. *Flags Through the Ages and Across the World.* New York: McGraw-Hill, 1975.

Spiller Harry. *Death Angel: A Vietnam Memoir of a Bearer of Death Messages to Families.* Jefferson, NC: McFarland and Co., 1992.

Steffen, Randy. *The Horse Soldier, 1776-1943,* Norman: University of Oklahoma Press, 1978.

Stewart, Robert. *The Corps of Cadets: A Year at West Point.* Annapolis: Naval Institute Press, 1996.

Roosevelt, Theodore, Jr. and Grantland Rice. *Taps: Selected Poems of the Great War,* Garden City, NY: Doubleday, 1932.

Tunis, Edward. *Colonial Craftsmen and the Beginnings of American Industry.* Cleveland: The World Publishing Company, 1965.

Tunis, Edwin. *Colonial Living.* Cleveland: The World Publishing Company, 1957.

Tunis, Edward. *Wheels: A Pictorial History.* Cleveland: The World Publishing Company, 1955.

Urwin, Gregory J.W. *The United States Cavalry: An Illustrated History.* London: Blandford Press, 1983.

Van Doren, Carl, ed. *The Literary Works of Abraham Lincoln,* New York: Press of the Readers Club, 1942.

Weisberger, Bernard A. *Many People, One Nation.* Houghton Mifflin, 1987.

Whitehill, Walter Muir and Norman Kotker. *Massachusetts: A Pictorial History.* New York: Charles Scribner's Sons, 1976.

Williams, Peter W. *Houses of God: Region, Religion and Architecture in America.* Urbana: University of Illinois Press, 1997.

Wormser, Richard. *The Yellowlegs: The Story of the United States Cavalry.* Garden City, NY: Doubleday, 1966.

Yedinak, Stephen M. *Hard to Forget: An American with the Mobile Guerrilla Force in Vietnam.* New York: Ivy Books, 1998.

Acknowledgements

A wonderful community has developed during the creation of *Remembrance* and, in so many ways, made it possible. We are deeply grateful to each of you.

We would like to thank our production team.

Rufus Collinson and Jim Wright for editing and proof reading. Rufus and Jim volunteered their time as a tribute to important veterans in their lives. Jim salutes three WW II veterans – his father, the late Army Capt. John S. Wright; his mother, Navy Nurse Margaret Bowers [Wright]; and his friend, the late Navy Lt. J.G. Thomas Finn. Rufus remembers her father Edward A. Johnson who served in WW II and her good friend David Nudenberg who was killed Vietnam.

Mike Celizic for his writing assistance

Tom Lennon for art direction, typography and technical direction and Sandy Lennon for technical assistance

Colonel Ronald E. Elliott (U.S. Army ret.) for military history fact checking

Peter Ciresa of Tech Photo & Imaging for producing the color/black and white transparency prints

David Humphrey and Cari DeLaCruz of Integrated Communications for printing recommendations and coordination.

John Bettick of the National Museum of Funeral History for help with 19th century funeral facts

Jane Fletcher Naples for mounting and framing artwork

Louis Simpson, WWII veteran and Pulitzer Prize poet, for his incredible poetry and invaluable contribution

Irene Carlisle for her poignant poem and her daughter Jo Ellen Zembsch for her gracious generosity

We would like to thank the following people for their invaluable support:

Congressman Benjamin A. Gilman, WWII

Dr. Richard W. Hull, professor of history New York University

Robert J. Fabrizio, Vietnam War, Commander of the Nicholas P. Lesando Jr. American Legion Post 214, Warwick, NY,

Fellow Legionnaires at Nicholas P. Lesando Jr., American Legion Post 214, Warwick, NY

John Fahey, Korean War, Commander, Veterans of Foreign Wars of the U.S. Warwick Post 4662, Warwick, NY and all the members

Rev. Dr. Duncan T. Trueman, WWII, Chaplain 106th Infantry Division

Deputy Chief Joe Di Bernardo, Vietnam War, Division Commander 6th Division FDNY

David M. Reel, Curator, West Point Museum United States Military Academy

Congressman Walter B. Jones, Third District, State of North Carolina for his support

Senator Thomas P. Morahan, Korean War, 38th District, State of New York

LaMar Williams, Director of Association Development, Children's Miracle Network, Salt Lake City, Utah

Assemblyman Howard D. Mills, 95th District State of New York

Richard K. Kolb-Publisher, Director of Publications and Editor in Chief VFW Magazine

Russell M. Long, Chaplain (LTC-Ret) US Army

Pastor David Lipsy, Heritage Reformed Congregation

J. Richard Gessell, Korean War, Business Partner

Jerry Donnellan, Director Veterans Service Agency, County of Rockland, NY

Evelyn Struck Walsh and Rose Struck Milstein for their encouragement, advice and poetry

David Hultgren, Librarian, Albert Wisner Library

Captain Kevin Doell, US Army Intelligence

Lieutenant Joe Berry, NYC Fire Department

Phil and Penny Potter

Dr. René Barendregt, Lethbridge University, Alberta

Ralph Vander May

Mark Jacobus

And, of course, we want to especially thank Betty Fletcher for her patience and her love.

Rob, we have shared a unique and most rare experience working together as son and father producing *Remembrance*. Your talent developing concepts and knowing what to write and how to write it - is your gift. We both are sensitive about the subject and that shines forth in manuscript and art.

What would we have done without Rufus considering all her suggestions and thorough editing; I cannot imagine. You have been invaluable, Rufus, and we express our great appreciation.

Thank you Rob for being who you are.

Dad, we have been able to do what most people only dream of. I will carry memories of working together on *Remembrance* with me all my life. Your love of rough-hewn beauty, the simple, the old, the small, all things American shines through in each painting and drawing that comes from your hand and your heart. Growing up surrounded by your patient, careful dedication to your art has helped me to find the courage to devote my life to mine. It is an honor and always an inspiration to be your son.

With malice toward none; with charity for all; with firmness in the right, as God gives us to see the right, let us strive on to finish the work we are in; to bind up the nation's wounds; to care for him who shall have borne the battle, and for his widow, and his orphan — to do all which may achieve and cherish a just, and lasting peace, among ourselves, and with all nations.

—Abraham Lincoln, Second Inaugural Address

I think it is a noble and pious thing to do whatever we may by written word or moulded bronze and sculpted stone to keep our memories, our reverence and our love alive and to hand them on to new generations all too ready to forget.

–Captain Oliver Wendell Holmes, 20th Massachusetts

And so, my fellow countrymen, today I report to you that your sons and daughters have served you well and faithfully with the calm, deliberated determined fighting spirit of the American soldier, based upon a tradition of historical truth as against the fanaticism of an enemy supported only by mythological fiction. Their spiritual strength and power has brought us through to victory. They are homeward bound — take care of them.

Douglas MacArthur

— General Douglas MacArthur, address to the American people
after the Japanese surrender at the end of World War II

About the Artist

Robert A. Fletcher is a Korean War veteran, United States Army Infantry who served with the German Occupational Forces as a corporal in the 69th Infantry Regiment Headquarters Company liaison.

After the war, Bob became a general partner in the Fletcher-Walker-Gessell Advertising Agency. He worked there as a technical illustrator and corporate client planner for advertising programs, presentations and government proposals. Bob's technical illustrations have appeared in magazines throughout the world, including *Aviation Week, Flight Magazine* and *Jane's Armament Books.*

Bob has had a great respect and reverence for veterans since he was a child. He says, "I learned about the military through parades, funerals and books. This fascination has remained with me."

After leaving the agency, Bob found the opportunity to deeply explore this interest, "I was determined to use my God-given talent for visual communication to refresh our memories of our veterans and their families." This was the beginning of *Remembrance* and the fulfillment of a lifetime passion.

Bob paints in a reconstructed barn overlooking a pond on his farm in the hamlet of New Milford in New York's Hudson Valley. Bob and his wife Elizabeth have four children and they enjoy spending time with their eight grandchildren.

Bob is a member of the Nicholas P. Lesando Jr. Warwick American Legion Township Post 214 and Veterans of Foreign Wars Post 4662 Warwick, New York.

About the Author

Robert B. Fletcher is the author of *Blues Harmonica for Beginners* and *Blues Grooves for Guitar* (Alfred Publications). He is also the author of the *Gospel Harmonica Workbook* and *Kim Wilson: My Blues* (both from Kevin's Harps Publications).

A regular columnist for *American Harmonica Newsmagazine, Harmonica World,* and a contributor to *Zip Lines: The Voice of Adventure Education,* Fletcher's work has been published in a variety of music magazines and arts journals. He has been an instructor at the National Guitar Workshop for over a dozen years and has taught and performed with two-time Grammy Award nominee and W.C. Handy Award winner Ronnie Earl.

Rob is also a corporate teambuilding consultant and is trained as a Wilderness First Responder. He holds a BA in Music performance from the State University of New York at New Paltz and lives on Cape Ann in Massachusetts.

Remembrance: A Tribute to America's Veterans

Supporting Organizations

The American Legion is comprised of 2.7 million members. These wartime veterans, working through 15,000 community-level posts, dedicate themselves to God and Country and traditional American values: strong national security; adequate and compassionate care for veterans, their widows and orphans; community service; and the wholesome development of our nation's youth.

The Veterans of Foreign Wars of the United States is comprised of 1.8 million members belonging to 12,000 community level posts. VFW members are devoted to ensuring national security, assisting disabled veterans and promoting Americanism through education.

Remembrance: A Musical Tribute to America's Veterans

Enrich your *Remembrance* experience with the greatest military and patriotic music from America's rich history compiled for the first time on CD. Explore the inspiring sounds of America, from the Revolutionary War to today. You will find sensitive, moving, and original renditions of such classics as "God Bless America," "Rally 'Round the Flag," "I'll Be With You in Apple Blossom Time," "Dixie," "America the Beautiful," "Johnny Has Gone for a Soldier," and many others. All are arranged and performed by a unique group of musicians featuring classical guitar, harmonica, acoustic slide guitar, upright bass, and mandolin. *Remembrance: A Musical Tribute to America's Veterans* is available either with the book or separately for $14.99 plus $2 shipping and handling.

Iron Mountain Press

Sales and Distribution Offices: PO Box 7, New Milford, New York 10959
Phone: 845-986-9861   Fax: 845-988-9915   Website: www.veterantribute.com
Remembrance: A Tribute to America's Veterans is available via mail order.
Prints of selected paintings are also available in a variety of formats. Please write to the above address or visit www.veterantribute.com for more information.

Iron Mountain Press books are available at special discounts for bulk purchases, for sales promotions, fund-raising, or educational purposes.